Nottingham...
The Sinister Side

CRIME AND PUNISHMENT 1864-1964

by **Steve Jones**

INTRODUCTION

After completing six books on crime and social history in my native London, I determined to turn my attention to the same themes in my adopted home town of Nottingham.

From the day I unearthed the excellent archive photographs of villains at the turn of the century, I have been astonished at the amount of unpublished information dealing with all matters of policing, crime and social history that is waiting to hit the presses.

Trawling the records at Nottingham University, The Local Studies Library, Nottingham Archives, The Public Record Office and The National Newspaper Library, I unearthed detailed accounts as to how harsh life must have been for many of the city's inhabitants, especially in the early years covered by the book.

When reading accounts and looking at photographs of a particular period you become engrossed, you live the times. I quickly became a time traveller. Thus I was in court with 'Nurse' Waddingham; I lived in the filthy conditions of Narrow Marsh; I witnessed the execution of John Brooks and sought pleasure in the Victorian brothels. I had a fascinating time!

If you are a time traveller, interested in crime, and, dare I say, the causes of crime, please join me in the stories of the hundred years from the last public execution in Nottingham (1864) to the last hanging in Britain (1964).

Please travel with me to Nottingham...the Sinister Side.

First published in 1996 by
Wicked Publications
222, Highbury Road,
Bulwell,
Nottingham NG6 9FE
England.
Telephone: (0115) 9756828

ISBN 1 870000-06-4

By the same author:

LONDON...THE SINISTER SIDE

WICKED LONDON

LONDON THROUGH THE KEYHOLE

CAPITAL PUNISHMENTS

IN DARKEST LONDON

WHEN THE LIGHTS WENT DOWN

see pages 103-104

Typeset and printed in Great Britain by
J. W. Brown (Printers) Limited, Darwin Press
77a Blackheath Road, Greenwich, London SE10 8PD
Telephone: 0181-691 1357

CONTENTS

NOTTINGHAM'S LAST PUBLIC EXECUTION

8 a.m. Wednesday, 10th August 1864 - the end of the Fiskerton murderer

The barricade immediately in front of the county hall was entered by the crowd about half-past five o'clock, at which time the arrangements had been completed. Many of those who filled the doors from the County Police-station to St. Mary's church gate had been there all night, and the rush that took place when the central barricade was thrown open was fearful...

The crowd presented the appearance which is peculiar to executions. Amid the roughs whose loud ribald shouts fell like mockery on the ear, might be seen here and there women, who must have been devoid of that delicacy which belongs to the sex.

There might also be seen more respectable members of society impelled to witness the execution by motives of curiosity. Ever and anon loud shouts of mirth and laughter rent the air, caused by the rough pranks practised upon those who showed an obstinacy in preserving order, or, upon the police officers in front of the palisades. Bonnetting was the favourite amusement, against which there was no resource but to remove the hat. One man had the lining of his hat torn out and this was the signal for another burst of excitement.

1. A very early photo of the Shire Hall circa 1870, some six years after Parker's execution.

The windows of the County Tavern and the warehouses on either sides were crowded by spectators. At half-past seven o'clock the High Pavement from St. Mary's Church to the Town Hall was one sea of faces, of every class and description of society, among whom might be observed also a number of butchers, the fraternity to which the prisoner belonged...

It was computed that at least 10,000 persons were now present. The scaffold and the drop with its ghastly surroundings now became the object of every person's attention and conversation. The scaffold was surrounded by a boarding about four feet in height, thus preventing the mob from seeing the culprit after the drop had fallen.

A number of religious persons had the bad taste to parade among the crowd, displaying placards headed "Jesus only" "Set your house in order," "Eternity's at hand" &c. Members of the crowd addressed these men in rather jocular terms, but it is fair to say that they answered with great moderation, reminding their hearers of the salvation of the thief on the cross.

At about ten minutes to eight o'clock a hush prevailed in the immense crowd caused by one of the superintendents of police announcing that the procession was leaving the gaol. At once the people at the front raised their hats, presenting with their bare heads and unified countenances a sight wonderful to witness. A feeling of painful expectation and dread ran through the hearts of all and many faces were blanched by the thought of the awful spectacle about to be gazed upon.

Still some portions of the eager mass of spectators continued to indulge in practical jokes, maltreating policemen, and raising one another on their shoulders.

The eyes of all were now directed with anxious gaze at the scaffold, every moment increasing the excitement.

At two minutes before eight the excitement was too intense to be described. Another two minutes and an awful hushed cry ran through the assembled mass, the cause of it being the arrival of the procession from the condemned cell...

2. Nottingham's most famous own goal. The stonemason had to correct his spelling mistake outside one of the entrances to Shire Hall.

3. An early wood carving of an execution outside Shire Hall. Large crowds from all walks of society gathered and there was a carnival atmosphere with hats and bonnets being thrown into the air whilst the mob awaited the arrival of the condemned man.

Exactly at eight o'clock Mr. J.T. Brewster, the acting under-sheriff, first made his appearance on the scaffold, followed by the Reverend W. Howard, the chaplain, and the governor. Next came the culprit accompanied by one of the turnkeys, and the person who had been sitting up with him, and last of all the hangman.

The chaplain and the under-sheriff took their place on the right hand side of the convict, whilst the turnkey and the officers stationed themselves on the right. The culprit was neatly dressed in a suit of dark tweed. Immediately on setting foot on the scaffold he engaged in prayer most earnestly for a few moments, during which the crowd below was hushed in complete silence, broken only by the sobs of women.

The culprit then stood firmly forward underneath the fatal drop, and looking straight in front of him, as if his thoughts were in the other world, prepared himself for the hangman. He looked haggard and nervous, but he was evidently engaged in prayer to his Saviour. His lips slightly moved in prayer but no audible words escaped from his mouth.

Askern then commenced the fatal task of putting on the white cap and adjusting the noose. Immediately upon these preparations the condensed feelings of the crowd betrayed themselves by shouts of "Townley" which was taken up a few moments but died away. The culprit stood very firmly whilst the noose was adjusted, his pinioned arms being raised in front. His hands twitched nervously, turning a blue colour, whilst his breath came in long gasps. The hangman, a tall muscular man, with bushy black whiskers, streaked with grey, performed his awful task with despatch, the blanched faces of the crowd below being a sight to dwell for ever on the minds of those who saw it. The hangman then retired to draw the bolt.

"In the midst of life we are in death."

At the moment these words were uttered by the chaplain the bolt was drawn with a terrible sound, and a sensible shudder ran through the crowd, many of the women shedding tears, whilst the mob in front of the hall made a partial rush to the scaffold shouting "Townley." The scene was awfully exciting, yells, and shouts of "Townley" continuing. The culprit meanwhile gave several convulsive quivers, and after some struggles which lasted rather longer than usual, his soul was launched into eternity. The crowd swayed to and fro, anxious to get a glance at the body but were unable to do so in consequence of the boarding.

In the course of a few minutes the crowd began to move away, and so terminated the last sad act of the Fiskerton drama.

After hanging on the gallows an hour, the body was cut down and interred in the burial ground within the precinct of the gaol.

The Nottingham Journal 11.8.1864

The death of Richard Thomas Parker, aged 29, represented the final act in a matricidal drama that began with the drunken shooting of both his parents. Richard, the sole after-thought product of his mother's second marriage, was said to be so thoroughly indulged as to be beyond salvation. Certainly his penchant for over imbibing, whatever its cause, was the curse of his family's life and, ultimately, of his own.

In his cups, Richard Parker, like so many drunks before and after him, was prone to excessive violence. The culmination of this all too familiar story was a wild fire attack on both his parents after a drunken row with his father. Parker Senior survived, his wife was not so lucky. The former Miss Tutbury, of Bingham, died as the result of a vain attempt to save her husband from harm. She was 75 years old.

After August 10th 1864 all executions in Nottingham became private, enclosed affairs, witnessed only by a handful of officials. Exclusion from the gruesome spectacle did not see an end to civil curiosity, however - it was the rare execution that didn't capture public imagination - as we shall see with the case, thirteen years later, of another drunken murderer.

4. Murderers executed at the Shire Hall had quick lime added to their coffins and were buried under the slabs in the back yard. Richard Thomas Parker's headstone may be seen in front of the window in the second arch from the right. The initials are R.T.P. and not R.I.P.

'GOD REMEMBER ME'

The execution and dissection of the Lenton murderer - John Brooks.

In December 1877 a young man named Bentley, while crossing Lenton Sands, had his attention drawn by a wildly gesticulating figure. John Brooks, a handsome, church-educated 32-year-old lace-maker - who had recently taken to the bottle - swaggering and barely able to stand upright, blurted out, to a shocked Bentley, that he had just committed murder. Subsequently the police discovered, in a nearby hedge, the body of 23-year-old Caroline Woodhead. She had virtually been decapitated. A razor, drenched with blood, was found discarded close by.

5. A blood-soaked razor was discovered near the body of Caroline Woodhead.

Both John and Caroline had previously been married, to different partners, from whom they had separated. After a short spell working in Calais, the couple had returned together to live in Nottingham. Theirs was to be a brief affair.

The following account of the confession, execution and dissection of John Brooks was taken from a contemporary report in *The Owl* :

THE CONFESSION

I, John Brooks, now lying under sentence of death in the Borough Gaol, Nottingham, for the murder of Caroline Woodhead on Tuesday 11th December, 1877, do hereby make the following statement:-

I admit the justice of my sentence, but solemnly assert that the murder was not premeditated; it arose out of a disordered state of mind, the outcome of drink and trouble. Had the advice of my poor mother and friends been taken, I should have left for Calais on Thursday 6th December, whereas I got drunk and missed the train. On Friday I was drinking all though the day. On Saturday the 8th I accidentally met C.W. on the Long-row. When she saw me she came up to me and said:

"Oh, what, you're drunk."

During our conversation I told her that I was almost mad with one thing and another and that I intended cutting my throat. From this she strongly dissuaded me, urging me to try and get work and go to Long Eaton for the purpose. I left her with the promise that I should meet her, as she requested, at the top of Wellington Street, Derby-road, at 6.30. p.m. on Tuesday evening December 11th to tell her the result. During the remainder of Saturday I got more drunk.

On Sunday morning I went with a few friends to Hucknall Torkard to a club house where we stayed drinking all the day, and I slept in the town with a friend. On Monday morning I came to Nottingham and spent a portion of the day at the "Rutland Arms" in Parliament street. I then went and pawned my overcoat for drink. In the evening I strolled down to the "Leather Bottle" and there I sold my waistcoat. On Monday night I slept at the coffee house on Bunker's hill; when on dressing in the morning I first discovered a razor in my pocket, which I suppose I must have obtained in some way the night before, but how, when and where I know not. When in Calais C.W. and myself once found a razor in bed and never knew how it came to be there.

During Tuesday morning, December 11th, I visited some liquor vaults in Chapel Bar and elsewhere. I afterwards went to the "George and Dragon" to the back premises, when on taking the razor out of my pocket, it fell on the floor and broke from the handle. Through hearing a man come up the yard I hastily picked it up and thrust it into my pocket, and afterwards in "Perry's Vaults" wrapped it round with a part of my scarf. On going up the Derby-road I met an old friend who I expected to stop and talk with me, but seeing me drunk he shunned me. This exasperated me very much, and added considerably to my already unsettled state of mind. In due course I reached the Victoria Inn, New Radford, where I was drinking with one Falconbridge of Bulwell or Basford. On leaving him I walked up Wellington-street, and according to our Saturday's appointment met C.W. who came with a shawl over her head, and the first thing she said was:

"Why you're drunk again, and you haven't been to Long Eaton!"

I walked down to Mills-lane with her and waited there till she got her hat. We then went down into New Lenton, and called at a beerhouse, and asked for a glass of rum, but soon found out our mistake; (some pubs only sold beer) however, we each had a glass of ale. Thence we proceeded to the "New Inn" when we each had a glass of rum, standing at the tap board. Afterwards we walked round by the "Kean's Head" public-house, where just opposite C.W. put her arms round my body, and pushing her hand into my pocket, said:-

"What are you going to do with the razor; give it to me?"

I think she must have seen it in my side pocket, for my coat came unbuttoned at the "New Inn". We had a struggle, and she obtained possession of the razor; but after a time I got it back from her, and then both our hands were cut.

On reaching the corner of Mills-lane and the road to the Park, I bid her good-night and we parted, as she had been urging me to go to my sisters at Hyson-green for the night, as I had no money. Scarcely had I gone many yards when she came running after me saying:

"I know you will go to Nottingham, come with me and I will show you the nearest way to your sister's"

Hence our position in Back Avenue. When we were standing there I reiterated my determination to take my life, and we got to high words about it, as she she did not know what would become of

her, for she would rather die than live with her mother'. At this stage of the altercation she turned up her face toward me, and in a most impassioned way cried out;-

"No, Jack, no, kill me first, kill me first rather than that."

Then in a momentary fit of passion I plunged the razor into her throat, when we both immediately fell to the ground. I turned my head towards her at once and she said:-

"Oh Jack."

But I could catch no more for I heard a gurgling in her throat and saw her hand held up to it. This caused me much alarm, when it seemed to me the best thing to draw the razor across her throat again. After this I fainted away again for a short time, and on coming round again failed to find the razor to take away my own life as well. Being utterly distracted and not knowing what to do, I rushed out into Mills-lane and Derby-road, and for the rest it is well known, for it was sworn at the trial.

This is the truth, the whole truth and nothing but the truth, so far as I can remember of that dreadful crime, the murder of Caroline Woodhead, whom I

6. The last sad moments of Caroline Woodhead's life, literally cut short.

JOHN BROOKS THE ASSASSIN.

7. The murderer, in a drunken stupor, plunged the razor into his lover's throat in New Lenton.

dearly loved, and for which I shall soon have to suffer on the gallows. I have repented of all my sins, especially of the last, the greatest and most wicked of all, and I pray God of His infinite mercy to forgive me all for Christ's sake. Had it not been for the drink, the deed would never have been committed. Having had many companions who were kind-hearted and generous to a fault, but whose sin was like my own, a love of strong drink and continual attendance at the public-house, I hope my warning voice will not be lost upon them...

(Signed)   John Brooks.
Thursday, February 7th 1878.

THE EXECUTION

On Wednesday morning, Feb. 13th, at a quarter to eight o'clock, the tolling of the funeral bell announced that the very minutes of John Brooks, the Lenton murderer, were numbered.

Marwood had been in Nottingham all night, waiting to perform his third execution and earn his third ten sovereigns that week. The under-sheriff, several doctors, the officers of the gaol, and a few reporters were the only occupants of the debtor's yard where the scaffold was erected, the drop being level with the floor of the yard. The executioner suavely raised his hat as he passed to carefully examine the drop and fasten eight feet of rope to the cross beam. When the under-sheriff had delivered to him the warrant for the execution he folded his arms and waited.

Then the Rev. Mr. Dixon, the chaplain, in white surplice, and reading the English ritual, appeared at the head of a melancholy procession. First came the murderer - who had slept but four hours that night, and partaken of nothing but a cup of tea - between two warders. The deputy-governor of the gaol walked next, and he was followed by half a dozen turnkeys two and two.

Brooks, who was very good-looking, was neatly dressed, and had altogether made a careful toilet. His arms were tightly pinioned, but he walked firmly, with head erect, except the slight inclination towards the right shoulder which will be observed in his portrait. His face was pale but calm, and expressed neither fear nor bravado.

When placed on the drop, with the exception of one hasty glance downwards, when his legs were being pinioned by Marwood, his eyes were earnestly fixed on the sky, until the ghastly white cap was drawn over his face. 'O God, O Christ' he ejaculated in fervent tones, mingling his voice with that of the chaplain. Then as the rope was being adjusted he cried with incessant earnestness:

"God remember me."

CAROLINE WOODHEAD THE VICTIM

8. The 23-year-old paid the ultimate price for falling for a drunkard.

At eight o'clock the drop fell, and the black flag rose to tell the outside thousand that justice was satisfied. Life must have been extinct in a moment, for the rope did not even vibrate. It was a curious after-sight to see Marwood calmly wiping his face with a handkerchief and philosophically viewing the suspended corpse. The chaplain appeared very deeply affected, and a tear glistened in the eye of more than one hard-featured turnkey.

Tragic though these events were, what followed was, if anything, worse. The corpse was dragged by a rope from the pit below the drop and surgeons, impatient to dissect the body, did not even wait for the coroner's jury to view the deceased. In a flurry of almost orgiastic fervour they fell upon the flesh of the newly executed man.

THE DISSECTION

They [the coroners' jury] were met at the door by a surgeon with his sleeves turned up, and his hands, to the wrists, dyed in blood. Two other surgeons were there with ensanguined marks about their persons. The floor was streaked with blood. Surgical weights and scales were stained with gore. From the crimson hue of several buckets of water, it appeared to jurymen that the intestines of the deceased had been cleansed therein...Turning to the remains of the corpse, all but the face and a small portion of the neck were covered from view. The back of the head appeared to have been cut open, and from the flatness of the sheet in the region of the abdomen, jurymen believed that the internal organs had been removed.

EXECUTION OF JOHN BROOKS AT NOTTINGHAM

9. Brooks was executed at the Borough Gaol on February 13th 1878 and dissected by impatient surgeons a few hours later.

'LET THE BEAST BURN'

10. *The miserable Tucker looks on passively as his common-law wife burns after he doused her skirts with petrol and set them alight.*

Although John Brooks was guilty of Caroline's death, he at least showed remorse. This was certainly not the case with one of the vilest men ever to walk the streets of Nottingham: Joseph Tucker.

As today, so in Victorian times, domestic disputes culminating in violence frequently followed the loss of self-control through alcohol. After knocking back copious amounts of beer or gin couples would knock each other about. Husbands tended to use bare fists and heavy boots, while wives defended themselves with whatever came to hand, iron pokers and cutlery being two of the favoured weapons.

At under eight stone, Joseph Tucker packed a paltry punch, but what he lacked in power he made up for in ferocity: he was infamous for foul tempered brutality following drinking bouts. On 2nd May 1885, Tucker mounted a ferocious attack on Elizabeth Williamson, his common-law wife of nine years, subsequently telling a neighbour that he regretted not having killed her. One week later he did just that and in a manner cruel beyond belief.

On the evening of May 9th the 37-year-old shoe finisher, as was his wont, went drinking with Elizabeth. Inevitably the couple fell into heated argument. The habitues of Tucker's local Sneinton pub were no prudes, but they were truly shocked by the language Joseph employed on this occasion. He was said to have made use of some 'very shameful and shocking terms', one of which was described in the coroner's court as being 'of a most disgusting character.' (The coroner here took the opportunity of showing his abomination of this particular example of profanity by observing that of all the words in the English language which most deserved to be reprehended it was the one that the miserable Tucker so often resorted to. He, the coroner, regretted that it was used in Nottingham and the neighbourhood more so than in any district he knew. It wasn't 'duck').

After their altercation in the pub, the inebriated couple staggered back to their Trumpet Street home. That night Tucker went one stage further than the normal punching and kicking. As his wife slumped to the ground, from the combined effects of alcohol and battering, Tucker emptied the contents of a paraffin lamp over her wide skirts.

Then he callously set her alight.

THE HOUSE IN TRUPET ST.

11. The scene of the crime in Sneinton. The caption should read 'Trumpet Street'.

TAKING THE DEPOSITIONS OF THE DYING WOMAN

12. Elizabeth Williamson died from her burns one week after the assault.

William Savage, a neighbour, later gave testimony:

On the 9th of May I was at home and a little after 11 on the above night saw Williamson under one of the windows, resting on one knee. She was on fire and her clothes burning up. Tucker was there and when I entered Tucker was stepping back from the deceased to the wall...when deceased was blazing there was no-one else in the house but Tucker.
I said: "Oh, she's burning."
Tucker said: "Let the beast burn."

The witness then rushed off to fetch help. A short time later another neighbour arrived and noted that Tucker stood with his arms folded leaning against the pantry door casually watching his wife burn to death. A desperate young man threw a bucket of water over the burning woman but when asked to help, Tucker again replied, with his customary oath:

Let her burn.

Elizabeth was clutching onto life when she was finally admitted to hospital but died from severe burns seven days later. The coroner, a man of considerable experience, stated that 'a more brutal and abominable act could not have possibly been committed by any man'. He added that he had never heard of a more shocking case in his life. The juries at both the coroner's and high courts were horrified and unhesitatingly found Tucker guilty of wilful murder.

On 2nd August, Tucker was received into the Catholic church and baptised just twenty-four hours before he took the one way ticket to meet his maker. Many felt he deserved to burn in hell.

Several murders were executed by men 'of unsound mind', though whether the court accepted this plea depended a great deal on the judge. Henry Westby, unlike Tucker, was an intelligent, articulate young man, but he too shook the inhabitants of Nottingham on a night of double murder.

'OF UNSOUND MIND'

The double killing that horrified the populace of Nottingham in 1881.

Despite the heated arguments teenagers have with their often over-protective parents it is still thankfully rare that a father is shot dead by one of his offspring. It is rarer still for a murderer to *strengthen his nerve* by practicing on a work colleague. Such an event horrified the town of Nottingham in the winter of 1881.

The first body discovered - by his wife in their small tobacconists off St. Ann's Well Road - was that of 44-year-old Henry Westby. The first murder, however, had taken place some hours earlier, in Fraser's Solicitors' offices, Wheelergate. The victim, William Onions, did not live to see his fifteenth birthday. Both cold-blooded murders were committed by Henry Westby junior, aged 18.

Westby entered brandishing an iron bar. He swiftly stunned the boy with a heavy blow to the back of the head and then slashed wildly at his face and throat with a large fish knife. The wounds on Onions' bloodied arms showed how he had gamely fought for his life, screaming all the while. Nobody heard. The boy died of traumatic injuries to his neck and throat.

Leaving the floor soaked with his victim's blood, Westby left to buy a revolver. Returning to the scene of his butchery later that evening, the killer struck a match, checked that Onions was quite dead, then meticulously wiped the blood from the doorknob and locked up the office.

The deranged Westby, having proved his capacity to kill, then focussed his attention on the main object of his paranoid obsession: the murder of his own unsuspecting father.

THE DOUBLE MURDER IN NOTTINGHAM

CIGARS STATIONERY. WESTBY TOBACCONIST

THE ALARM

MURDER OF Mr WESTBY

13. Police arrive at the scene of the second murder at the small tobacconist's off St Ann's Well Road. Westby coldbloodedly shot his father who he believed to be forever finding fault with him.

A young curly-haired youth of above average intelligence, Westby worked in the same solicitor's office as William Onions. From the age of 16, Westby's mental health appeared to deteriorate. In the paranoid belief that other clerks were looking at him, Westby cut himself off from the rest of the office by erecting a screen. On the day of the murder, Onions was working alone, after hours.

After practising some time with his new weapon, the solicitor's clerk returned home. At 10 p.m. he calmly bade his family 'good night' and retired to bed. His parents followed an hour later. At 2.30.a.m., believing he had heard an intruder, Westby senior went downstairs to protect his property. At the inquest his wife, Elizabeth, took up the story:

I heard a loud report of firearms, and my husband, crying out that he was shot, staggered into the room. He said 'mind yourself' and then dropped down and died. I opened the window and called out. The police were first on the spot. My two girls came to me when the occurrence took place; but I did not see my son who had been sleeping in the top room. I never saw him in the house again.

MURDER OF THE BOY

14. The paranoid Henry Westby brutally murdered his 14-year-old work colleague William Onions to strengthen his nerve to kill his main intended victim, his own father.

Mrs. Westby did not witness her unstable son make good his escape after twice shooting his father. Ready and willing to shoot anyone who might have stood in his way, the young Westby fled into the night. The next day a massive search for the fugitive was instigated and a tight watch kept on the railway stations.

Henry Westby was eventually tracked down to a fowl house on Lenton Sands and persuaded to surrender. Throughout the inquest and ensuing trial he showed no emotion or remorse. He gave the impression of a surly, callous young man and when his mother broke down in court and rested her head on his shoulder he just brushed her away with the admonishment: *Don't be soft.* Westby admitted responsibility for both of the murders and stated that he had been planning to kill his father for some time. In his confession he said:

I am glad he is dead. I could not bear the sight of him. He is always finding fault with me.

If this grievance seems minor, consider the accused's justification for the murder of William Onions: *he was forever coughing, blowing his nose and spitting.* In truth, the murderer's main reason for killing his young colleague was to *strengthen his nerve* .

Prisoners in the nineteenth century rarely pleaded guilty to wilful murder as this invariably led to a meeting with Jack Ketch, whom nobody has met on more than one occasion. Westby stunned the court by pleading 'guilty' and it took his counsel some time to make him change his plea to 'not guilty'. They were looking for a verdict of 'unsound mind'.

It appeared that the defence had the flimsiest of cases. They argued that Westby slept in a hammock and did not often go out. A story about a trip to London eighteen months previously was also related. Here Westby was said to have been so miserable that he spent five hours in the waiting room of St Pancras Station. Beyond this, the only defence that could be put forward was that sane men do not kill their own fathers. In view of this inadequate defence Westby was, not surprisingly, found 'guilty' and sentenced to death. He showed no emotion whatsoever as he was led through the court trap door to the cells below.

It is doubtful whether the condemned man ever appreciated it, but his lawyer was a tireless, determined worker and, following an appeal, Westby was found to be of 'unsound mind'.

His sentence was duly commuted.

CAPTURE OF THE ASSASSIN

15. He was tracked down to a fowl house in Lenton Sands. Surprisingly for the times (1881) the death sentence was commuted on appeal.

WHIPPING BOYS

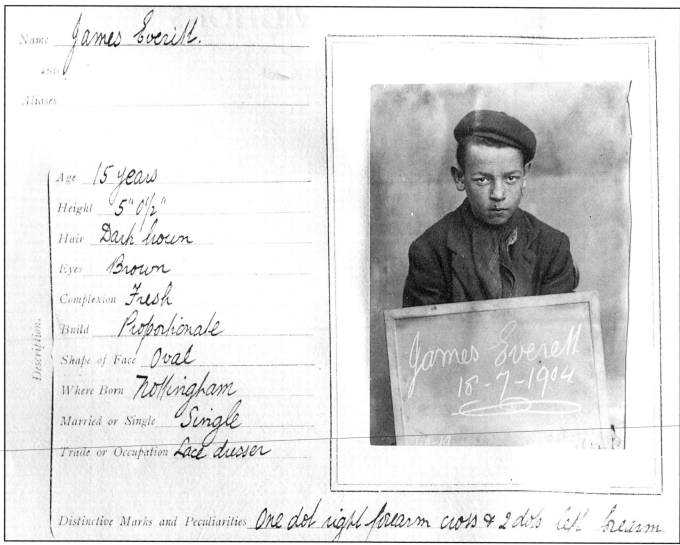

Name *James Everitt.*

AND

Aliases

Age *15 years*

Height *5" 0½"*

Hair *Dark brown*

Eyes *Brown*

Complexion *Fresh*

Build *Proportionate*

Shape of Face *Oval*

Where Born *Nottingham*

Married or Single *Single*

Trade or Occupation *Lace dresser*

Description.

Distinctive Marks and Peculiarities *One dot right forearm cross & 2 dots left forearm.*

16. James Everitt imprisoned for stealing rolls of newspaper.

A NEW PAIR OF WHISKERS

Besides stealing practically everything not nailed down, many young men and boys with time on their hands made a nuisance of themselves in other ways. As with the bus shelter today, in Victorian times the train station was the stopping point for those seeking a little light relief at others' expense. Youths would crowd around the entrances and exits, deliberately blocking the paths and jostling travellers under the guise of wishing to carry cases.

Places of worship were also a Mecca for maladjusted youths determined to challenge the established order. In July 1864 Samuel Chadwick, a young man 'unfavourably known to the police', was charged with using obscene language at Park Row Chapel. He asked a girl, Emma Barton (who coincidentally appeared in the same court on the same day charged with stealing a coat), whether she would lend him a hymn book. When she refused, he called her a 'foul' name and added his view that the chapel was only a ———. When one of the pew-openers remonstrated with him, Chadwick recommended that he *'get a new pair of whiskers'* - perhaps the Victorian equivalent of get a life? The prisoner and other delinquents had been turned out of the chapel on previous occasions and only came to play, not to pray. The Mayor, in charge of the court proceedings, questioned Chadwick as to his reasons for frequenting Park Row:

MAYOR: *Do you attend the chapel as a worshipper?*
PRISONER: *No Sir. I have never been inside it in my life. The witness told me I was a scamp.*
MAYOR: *No doubt you are.*

The prisoner's further statement that he went to chapel to see if he could get any benefit from it was greeted by laughter in the court. Nonetheless, Chadwick admitted that he had been a bad character but was now reformed. When told that he had to pay sureties of the peace for three months and the court costs the young man lost much of his swagger and feebly replied:

PRISONER: *I have nothing to pay with.*
MAYOR: *Then you will have an opportunity of attending [prison] chapel.*

SPARED THE ROD

Described as 'two little boys' William Samson and Thomas Goddard must have cursed their luck when they were caught stealing flowers from Mrs. Smith's Sneinton garden in 1864. They were apprehended by a bobby on the beat at 4 o'clock in the morning! The damage to the property and the flowers was estimated at 1d. but both boys were fined 5s. each, this having to be paid for by their parents.

In the same court, teenager Mary Lee was charged with stealing 4d. from the New Inn in Barrington. She was sentenced to 21 days hard labour. Another Mary, Mary Garratt, 9, served four days for stealing ten shillings, while 12-year-old Sarah Jane Nixon was sent down for two weeks for stealing her mother's clothes. Two of the youngest offenders to be imprisoned, for stealing iron, were a couple of likely lads from Bulwell. They were just seven years old. They were at least spared the rod.

In the 1870's the policy of whipping young offenders, to deter them from future lives of crime, was employed at the County Gaol. Most of the following offenders had no previous convictions but all were punished by flogging **and** custodial sentence. Only 8-year-old Joseph Streets and 11-year-old Benjamin had any previous convictions.

17. Albert Freeman had a particularly resilient rear end. 28 strokes of the birch did not deter him from thieving. Here photographed at the age of 19, he pursued a life of crime well into his twenties.

A 14-year-old was sentenced to 12 stripes for stealing a clothes line. The birch rod was made from a clutch of twigs bound together with stout twine at the handle. When the Home Office took responsibility for prisons in 1878 there were three categories of birch: thin, for juveniles up to 10; medium, for offenders 10-16, and thick for individuals over 16.

The birch was applied to naked buttocks, the prisoners' feet were kept together, their shirts lifted. A pad was sometimes introduced to the upper part of the thigh in the crutch to protect the scrotum if this was pendulous. For the most part little bleeding but much bruising was recorded.

The policy of flogging continued into the twentieth century with some of the young offenders developing particularly resilient backsides. One such young man, who rendered nonsensical the 'spare the rod' assertion, was the habitual offender Albert Freeman, here photographed as a 19-year-old. At 14, he received six strokes for stealing cherry brandy, followed a short time later by 10 for stealing two pigeons and the full dozen for purloining a pair of boots. They had little effect: whilst not yet 20, his list of misdemeanours almost matched his age and the young free man was destined to spend most of his life as anything but!

NAME	AGE	OFFENCE	DAYS
George Kirk	13	stealing pair of cuffs	(14)
David Marshall	13	stealing potato bags	(7)
Chris Marshall	14	stealing pigeons	(7)
William Slater	10	stealing a coat	(4)
William Wilkinson	12	stealing £2.10s	(7)
John Evans	10	stealing a bridle	(4)
Henry Clifford	12	stealing a bridle	(4)
Joseph Capley	14	stealing 2s and tobacco	(14)
Henry Coulson	14	intending to commit felony	(7)
Joseph Streets	8	shop breaking	(3)
Benjamin	11	shop breaking	(3)
George Hallam	9	stealing knives	(21)
William Rayner	12	stealing apples	(3)
Thomas Johnson	13	stealing a whip	(3)
Alfred (no surname)	13	stealing a chicken	(30)

BUSH DOES THE BIRD

In comparison, John Bush was a mere novice when he received six strokes for stealing a tin of condensed milk. Accordingly Bush branched out to the big time, acquiring cut flowers and clothes without paying. The annals are full of examples like this, with full details kept of young offenders:

NAME: JOHN BUSH.

AGE: 16

HEIGHT: 4' 10"

EYES: BLUE

COMPLEXION: FRESH

BUILD: SLIM

SHAPE OF FACE: OVAL

WHERE BORN: NOTTINGHAM

MARRIED OR SINGLE: SINGLE

TRADE OR OCCUPATION: COLLIER

ADDRESS: 16, BROUGHAM YARD

DISTINGUISHING FEATURES: TATTOO FLAG LEFT ARM.

18. John Bush aged 16. Four years previously he had received six of the best for stealing a tin of condensed milk. He proved the 'spare the rod' merchants wrong by re-offending in 1900 and was imprisoned for 14 days for stealing clothes to the value of 20s. 6d.

Children were often encouraged by their parents to steal from shops and pass the stolen goods on to them. In 1905 Mary Hayes (12) and Norah Borridge (11) were charged with stealing the following items from a shop in Goldsmith street; a tin of apricots, a tin of potted crab and a box of dates with a total value of 1s 6d. They faced a second charge of theft later on the same day, stealing a tin of herrings- discovered partly eaten- and other items from a second shop.

Annie Hayes, the mother of Mary, was charged with receiving the stolen goods in both cases. The mother entered a plea of 'not guilty' and the girls 'guilty'. Mary and Norah had been caught red-handed trying to steal some chocolate and when searched the other stolen goods were quickly discovered in Mrs. Hayes' home. Norah pointed to a cupboard where her friend's mother stashed the stolen goods. According to Norah the only maternal advice Mrs. Hayes passed on was:

Mind you don't get caught.

The bench stated that they had little doubt about the mother's guilt and reluctantly sent her to prison for one month. Both mother and daughter wept uncontrollably in each other's arms as Mr. Hayes begged the magistrates to reduce the punishment to a fine. They refused. The cases against the two girls were adjourned indefinitely with Mary Hayes being sent to an industrial school and Norah Borridge to a voluntary home.

BAD COMPANY

A case where a 12-year-old boy was hauled before the magistrates for theft left the learned gentlemen with a smile on their faces. When the defendant's father was questioned about his son's behaviour he replied:

He was formerly very good, but since he has joined a church choir he has been altogether different. I think it's the company he has got into. (laughter in court).

What! in the church choir?

Yes.

Being the boy's first offence the case was adjourned *sine die*.

FINED FOR FURIOUSLY RIDING A CYCLE

19. George Adams. A life of crime must have been stressful. George in the photo is only 20 years old.

Fines were imposed for minor offences to help keep the prison population down. The following examples were recorded in 1906:

Playing cards: one shilling.

Allowing child to beg: five shillings.

Using obscene language: ten shillings.

Chimney on fire: one shilling in poor box.

Not sending child to school: seven shillings and sixpence.

Throwing stones: two shillings and sixpence.

Playing pitch and toss: two shillings and sixpence.

Crying out for the purpose of selling on Sunday: two shillings and sixpence.

Spilling offensive matter: caution.

Furiously riding a bicycle: seven shillings and sixpence.

Selling ox tongue unfit for food: thirty shillings.

Applying false trade description to butter scotch: twenty shillings.

Selling milk with fat abstracted: forty shillings.

Selling cream containing boric acid: nine shillings and ninepence.

We can get some idea of the significance of these fines by comparing them with 1910 food prices:

Bread: 2d per loaf

Butter: 1 shilling per pound

Jam: 3d per pound

Tea: 6d per 6 ozs

Tin of milk: 4d

Haddock: 2d

Potatoes: 1 penny per 2 lbs

20-23. *Jane Riley, Frank Sage, Henry Thompson and George Simpson. In the early days of police photography (these photos date from 1884) offenders objected to having their photographs put on file. Before she was captured on film Jane Riley used the aliases Elizabeth Shepley, Annie Davis and Theresa Relekin. Another woman, Sarah Wilson would change her name as often, or probably more often, than she changed her dress. She would answer to the name of Emily Bremman, Emily White, Emily Camden, Emily Robinson, Emma Hurst, Clara Black, Nan McDonald, Emily Wood, Emily Smith and Emily Harris.*

All four offenders photographed here were charged with frequenting which broadly meant being found more than once in a location where you were likely to commit a breach of the peace; in illicit drinking clubs, brothels or at the races etc. The police used the law to evict undesirables from places such as the Railway Station.

24. *Rose Graham on 10th October 1904. Charged with stealing a purse and 6d she appears the worse for drink and very shy of the cameras.*

25. *Rose Graham five days later. The Dublin woman is still refusing to hold her name board. She was sentenced, rather harshly, to six months' imprisonment.*

26. *In the early days of police photography considerable force was needed to overcome the resistance of criminals no longer able to get away with using an alias.*

ROGUES' GALLERY

20.

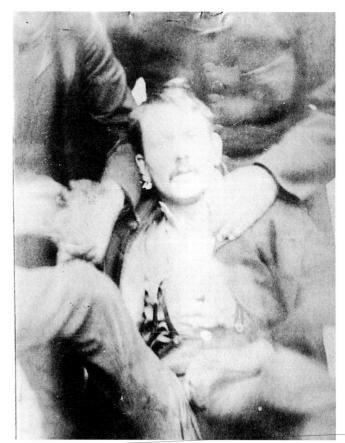

21.

22.

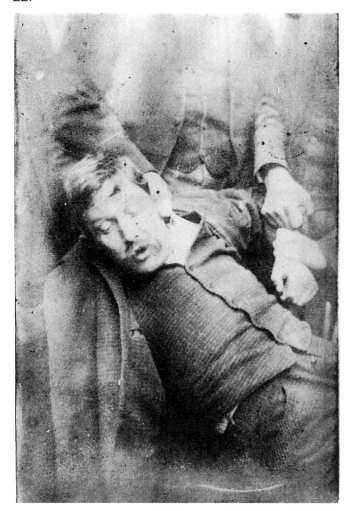

23.

24.

25.

26.

23 COURT APPEARANCES IN 23 YEARS

27. Ellen Steer from 19 Knob Yard, Narrow Marsh. The 23-year-old prostitute was no stranger to the court room having committed 22 minor offences for drunkenness and bad language. Described in court as being 'of a very low type' Ellen showed very little respect for anybody within the judicial system and was sentenced to four months' hard labour for stealing a drunken punter's wallet. Prison was little deterrent and Ellen continued to offend throughout her twenties and later specialised in stealing shoes and slippers.

Ellen Steer, an amiable, good-natured soul, was no stranger to the courts. A prostitute from Narrow Marsh, she showed scant respect for anybody in authority, her informal manner causing much amusement. Aged twenty-three, and appearing for the twenty-third time before the beak, she took the oath and spoke directly to the recorder, totally ignoring the jury:

Talk to them, said the recorder.

But I'm talking to you! Ellen replied and continued speaking as if she and the recorder were the only two present in court.

In July 1907, along with a fellow doxy, Loisa Harrison, Ellen was opportuning on Canal Street, hoping to find a drunken punter to fleece. He duly appeared in the form of the gullible Mr. Swanwick, who must have thought that his luck was in as the girls each placed an arm through his. Ellen surreptitiously inserted her hand into the drunkard's pocket - after the wad, not the cod - removed his purse, which contained two pounds, and passed it on to Loisa, who made her excuses and left, disappearing up Bishop's Yard to return a couple of minutes later. Presently the drunkard noticed his loss and called a policeman. A quick search of Bishop's Yard, by an intrepid P.C. Walters, resulted in the recovery of the missing money and the subsequent arrest of the two ladies of the night.

Back in the courtroom, Loisa Harrison wept uncontrollably in the dock.

What are you crying for? Ellen shouted to her friend. *You have nothing to cry for.*

Detective-Supt. Parnham said that the prisoners were of a very low type, and had several convictions for drunkenness and obscene language. Both were sent to prison for four months with hard labour. Undaunted, Ellen Steer doubtless proved a fillip to her fellow Bagthorpians!

GIVE A DOG A BAD NAME

28. Sarah Hodgkinson, a lady of the streets. Sentenced to one month's hard labour for stealing £2 from a customer.

Described by the *Evening Post* court reporter as a *'showily dressed woman'*, 24-year-old Sarah Hodgkinson specialised in stealing money from 'customers' whilst their minds and bodies were otherwise occupied. At 11.30.p.m. the prostitute picked up a traveller, Alfred Bertram, near the Caledonian Hotel. A price was agreed and the couple went to Sarah's room at 1a, Needle Place. As he put his trousers back on, Bertram found his purse was not in its usual pocket. He immediately became suspicious and upon examining the contents, found two sovereigns missing. Sarah denied taking the money and Bertram returned with a policeman in the early hours of the morning. Despite a thorough search of the room no trace of the money was ever discovered. In the absence of this evidence there seemed little chance of the charge sticking, but Sarah was still convicted - doubtless on the basis of reputation. She was ordered to pay a fine of 20 shillings or spend 14 days in prison.

MARY KENT, QUEEN OF THE RECIDIVISTS

29. Mary Kent's sad life is depicted in her long list of convictions. (p25)

A study of the police records of prisoners detained at Bagthorpe Prison would reveal a large number of recidivists like Mary Kent and roughly the same number charged just one or two times. Examination of Mary's record shows that she spent most of her life in gaol following her first offence at just nine years of age.

Her debut in a Nottingham court was as a 38-year-old hardened criminal. She used the aliases Mary Coyle and Catherine McClary but her scarred face and tattoos soon alerted police as to her true identity.

Upon arrival in Nottingham at the turn of the century, Mary teamed up with another pickpocket, Elizabeth Jamieson. Both set off to the Market Place in search of a victim. Augusta Peel was standing near the country produce stall when she felt a tug on her dress. Mary, if she went to school, obviously received no careers advice. Judging by her string of convictions she was not the most nimble-fingered of pickpockets and not adept at her chosen profession. As if by reflex Augusta desperately felt for her purse but only grabbed fresh air. Her three shillings and sixpence had been stolen and the only two people who had been near her were Mary and Elizabeth.

An eye-witness told a policeman (they used to be there when you needed one) that she saw Mary insert her hand into Augusta's pocket whilst Elizabeth extended her cloak to hide the theft from other shoppers.

It seemed a relief for Mary to be caught as when she was challenged by Detective Hayward she compliantly replied:

Yes, I shall plead guilty.

Elizabeth Jamieson denied knowing Mary.

I don't know this woman. I know nothing at all about it.

Both women were sent to prison for one month.

30. As the record shows she spent most of her life 'inside' and almost seemed relieved when arrested for picking pockets in 1900. On the one arm she had the letters VALR tattooed and on the other MWMTKGIELEG.

PREVIOUS CONVICTIONS.

252.E.

Date.		Place.	Offence.	Sentence.
25 Jan	1871	Glasgow	Theft	Admonished.
13 May	1871	do	do	10 days & 3 yrs Refmy.
26 Feb	1875	do	do	60 days
8 Oct	1875	do	do	30 do
31 Nov	1875	do	do	60 do
19 June	1876	do	do	60 do
28 Aug	1876	do	do	60 do
26 June	1877	do	do	60 do
" "	"	do	do	60 do
13 Feb	1879	do	do	30 do.
13 Oct	1879	do	do	6 Months.
21 Dec	1880	do	do	6 do.
18 Oct	1882	do	do	5 Years
26 June	1886	do	do	5 do
8 Oct	1891	Paisley	Prevention C. Act	6 Months.
19 Apl	1892	Liverpool	Picking pockets	Rem & discharged.
3 July	1893	Wigan	Theft	6 Months.
21 Dec	1894	Liverpool	Picking pockets	Rem 7 days
18 Oct	1896	Birmingham	Attempting to pick pockets.	No appce Bailed.
19 July	1900	Nottingham	Attempt to steal purse & 9/6½ from person	1 Month
" "	"	do	Loitering with intent to commit a felony	No order
18 Aug	1900	Birmingham	Larceny	Discharged
31 Dec	1900	Stockton-on-Tees	Frequenting as Catherine McClosky.	3 M. H. L.
30 Sept	1901	Nott'm Sessions	Larceny from person.	15. M. H. L. Mary Faulkner
23rd Feby	1904	Glasgow	attempt to steal	15 Mos.
		Wakefield Ct. Sess.	Attempting to pick pockets	
25 Oct	05	Chester-le-Street	Loitering	1 Month H.L
15 Jan	07	York	Attempted larceny from person	2 years H.L
8 Apl	10	Blackburn Sess	Larceny from person	4 Months

A FAMILY AFFAIR

31. Harriet Turner stole £100 from her brother and planned to elope with her soldier sweetheart, Herbert Marshall.

Harriet Turner was so besotted with her soldier boyfriend that she stole a trunk containing £100 from her brother and fled the family home in Radford. She planned to marry Herbert Marshall from the Notts and Derby regiment and live on the stolen money. The full details of the case were revealed in court in September, 1904.

Frank Turner left a tin trunk containing £100 in gold, a suit of clothes, a pair of boots and other effects in his room. Returning home one Saturday afternoon at 1.30., he found his room and the house empty. Both his trunk and sister were missing. It did not need the mind of Sherlock Holmes to work out that if he found one he would probably find the other. Frank went straight to a second sister's house in Cambridge street and asked Elizabeth when she had last seen their sister, Harriet. When told that she had been there a few hours earlier and had asked to leave a trunk in the front room the frantic young man breathed a little more easily.

Upon inspection Frank found that his clothes and boots had been replaced with army issue and £35 of the gold was missing. When the thieves returned to Cambridge Street they were met by Detective Sergeant Drury and could not deny the charge;

Marshall was wearing the stolen suit and Harriet had in her possession some of the missing gold, a watch and chain and a gold wedding ring they had bought with the money.

The theft had been impulsive and the loving couple had not considered the consequences of their actions. Pleading guilty, Herbert Marshall was sentenced to four months' imprisonment. Harriet had two months to contemplate the folly of her ways.

32. The couple were caught red-handed and Marshall was sentenced to four months gaol and Harriet, two. This ended Harriet's life of crime but Herbert, who had three convictions for indecent exposure, was later gaoled for housebreaking and assault.

GYPSY LEE PROMISES THE EARTH

The magistrates' court was offered some light relief in 1907, when a gullible domestic servant brought a charge against a gypsy fortune-teller.

Elizabeth Lee was on the knock in Barrack Lane, on the edge of the Park Estate off Derby Road. Ostensibly selling lace, the 37-year-old also did a sideline in fortune telling. Maggie Sharp, the aggrieved domestic servant, refused the lace, but when offered the prospect of seeing what the future held, at half-price, opened out her hand with an air of expectation and excitement. Elizabeth pocketed the shilling fee and gravely set to work on Maggie's palm:

You will leave this house and go in a hurry. Next time you are paid you will give in your notice....

Some ten minutes later, with the 27-year-old servant still trying to take in the imminent changes to her life, Elizabeth enquired how much money Maggie kept in the house. The foolish maid gave a detailed reply: a half sovereign, with a further six shillings in silver and copper. The gypsy then asked for additional money so the prediction would come true:

You must give me the silver and coppers. I shall want that to put on the planet to set it working. (Laughter in court).

Maggie handed over the six shillings (sharpish) neatly wrapped up, and was duly told that the money would be returned at a quarter-to-five. Here one of the magistrates, Mr. Acton, interrupted the story, which was proving to be an agreeable diversion from the usual humdrum cases of drunken brawls and petty theft:

Was that all, nothing about a dark man and a fair man?

She said I should have some money left me. I should go into business and do well after marriage. I was going to be married within six weeks.

She was right about the money leaving! Elizabeth returned from her van in Dunkirk and told Maggie that the money she had already handed over was not heavy enough, she needed the remaining ten shillings to make the prediction come true. Undaunted, Maggie handed over the rest of her savings. Three days later, Elizabeth made her first mistake.

Quite why the gypsy returned to the house three nights later is unclear, she should have known the well was dry. Maggie had smelt a rat and immediately asked for her money back. She was told Elizabeth did not have it. When questioned as to why she would not return the savings, Elizabeth replied:

If I take the ten shillings off I might as well take it all off. It will undo all the work that I have been doing in the planets the last three nights.

Maggie contacted the police. Elizabeth's own immediate future duly became crystal clear: if she didn't pay the thirty shillings fine she would spend the next twenty-one days in gaol. As for Maggie, it's highly unlikely that she married within the following six weeks and a racing certainty that she didn't do well in business.

THE DISAPPEARING RABBIT

Whilst doing her weekly shopping in Bulwell, Sarah Officer noticed three drunken teenagers, two girls and a boy, acting suspiciously (how little times change in this part of Nottingham). She saw the boy 'lift' some meat from the fishmonger's shop and immediately alerted the owner:

He has taken a rabbit.

Samuel Merchant hurried from the back of his shop to apprehend the thief. Rushing into the street he spotted Frank Mead and two teenage girls making off with what they hoped would be their supper. The shopkeeper managed to retrieve his rabbit (value one shilling), the thief, non too bright, reluctantly returning it with the words:

It is only a bit of gammon.

Bereft, and with an empty stomach, Frank sought to take his frustration out on someone who would

33. Gypsy Elizabeth Lee would promise the world when her palm was crossed with silver. She went on the knock looking for gullible domestic servants...and invariably found them.

not fight back. Who better than the woman who had alerted the shop-keeper? Approaching Sarah Ann Officer, the drunken coward punched her square on the mouth with such force that her two front teeth were knocked out. The two girls, Frank's sister Alice and one Annie Anderson, then further assaulted the bleeding woman, shouting abuse, whilst Frank pulled her nose. Alice showed little respect for the court and did not even bother to take out her curlers. Frank, whose only defence was that he was drunk, was imprisoned for one month and the two girls fourteen days apiece.

35. John Birch of 10, Temple Place, Narrow Marsh. A typical professional thief from the slum area of the city with 39 convictions for stealing. He would lift anything he could get his hands on, the booty including: fowls, a jacket, a shawl, boots, a barrow, a bag of coal, a bag of corn etc..etc.

36. George Roberts at 74 looks extremely fit on the prison diet he has become accustomed to over the years. He committed his first offence in 1845 when 14. A professional housebreaker he never changed his ways despite the lengthy spells in prison. In 1888 he was sentenced to 10 years. In 1904 he served 12 months hard labour in Nottingham. He died in prison eight years later.

34. Alice Mead from Bulwell showed scant respect for the court appearing in her curlers. She was sentenced to 14 days for a cowardly assault on a woman.

37. Guillaume Levarez, sentenced to six months for assault.

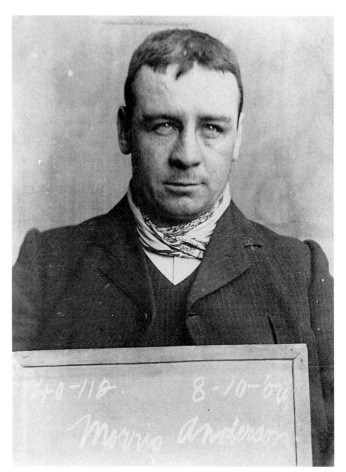

38. Mario Anderson, sentenced to one day's imprisonment for stealing a pipe.

39. James Kelly spent 21 days in Bagthorpe for stealing a raincoat.

40. Thomas Wilson, a pock marked hard man. 12 months hard labour in 1901 for G.B.H.

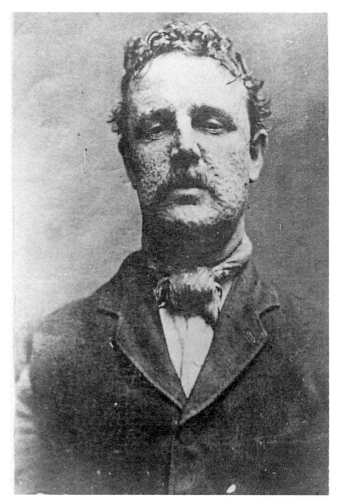

STEALING BOOTS, BODICES AND BOXES OF FISH

A study of 50 crimes perpetrated in 1908.

The printed details of 50 offenders (p32-33) were chosen entirely at random to illustrate the nature of crime on the streets of Nottingham in the early part of this century. Some culprits offended, or were caught, only once; others spent most of their lives in and out of prison. Let's take a more detailed look at some of the offenders.

41. Elizabeth Mart aka Smart. (No 9 in the chart) a prostitute from Leicester who specialised in picking the pockets of her clients. The 17-year-old was sentenced to two months with hard labour.

Elizabeth Smart (no.9) and John Woodward (no.10) both hailed from Leicester. At 18, Elizabeth was one year younger than her companion but certainly a lot wiser and more experienced in the criminal underworld. The labourer and his prostitute girlfriend took up residence in Riley's common lodging house in Narrow Marsh, where the emphasis was on the word 'common'. Elizabeth worked the pubs as a prostitute but made more money stealing from drunken clients.

After sharing a few bevvies with the teenage temptress, Isaiah Casterton, a lace-maker from Daybrook, noticed that his forty shilling watch and chain had disappeared. Elizabeth had swiftly passed on the booty to her accomplice, John, who was so anxious to unload the hot property that he offered the watch for sale outside Truman's Vaults, from where it had been stolen. It was shown to a labourer, Henry Davidson, who had been in the pub, but he declined the offer of the cheap timepiece and instead followed Woodward back to his lodgings. He then informed the police.

Because of her 'bad character', Elizabeth was sentenced to two months hard labour in Bagthorpe. John Woodward's mother came to the court to plead for her son, whom, she said, had fallen in with bad company and been led astray (well she would, wouldn't she?). He was sentenced to just one month. Henry Davidson, for his honesty, was given a monetary grant.

Two days later, another resident of the Narrow Marsh lodging-houses appeared in the same court. Thomas Knight (no.13) admitted stealing a pair of cheap boots (5s 11d.) from a shop in Beastmarket Hill. He had been spotted secreting the footwear under his coat by one P.C. Sykes and was duly sent down for a fortnight. On his way to the Guildhall the prisoner lamented the fact of having been charged with the theft of rubbish - clearly his street cred. was at risk!

Herbert Shipley (no 15) and Alfred Tomlinson (no 16) were hardly cut out for a life of crime. Shipley at the age of 16 was just 4' 4" tall and his accomplice, one year older, measured in at 5'. Arriving from Derby, the two boys tried to earn some pennies selling matches. With business slow, the youngsters decided to chance their arm at crime. P.C. Fisher noticed Herbert standing suspiciously on Derby Road. When searched the lad had difficulty explaining how he came to be in possession of a bodice and eight pairs of lady's collar supports with a retail value of 3s. 8d. The two menaces to society were hauled before the court where the elder, Alfred Tomlinson, gave details of their master crime:

I stole the things while Shipley looked for a policeman.

Shipley duly obliged and found one. Both boys were sentenced to one year's probation.

42. The master criminal Herbert Shipley (No.15). The 16-year-old at 4ft 8ins was part of the Derby mafia sent to terrify the inhabitants of Nottingham in 1905. Herbert was stopped by a policeman and found to have secreted about his body a bodice and eight pairs of ladies' collar supports. He was put on probation for one year.

An uncommon act of compassion was shown when another 16-year-old, Percy Thompson (no.23), appeared in court. Percy, a carter from Old Basford, pleaded guilty to stealing property to the value of £3 from his employer. As it was his first offence his boss was willing to drop the charge and subsequently re-hired the fortunate young man.

Martha Smith (no.24), a 45-year-old charwoman from Deering Street (off Wilford Road), specialised in stealing footwear. Arrested for stealing two pairs of boots, the police searched her room and discovered another 37 pairs, together with 11 pairs of slippers. The Meadows answer to Imelda Marcos duly spent the next three months at hard labour in Bagthorpe Gaol.

Two visitors to the city, Thomas Thompson (no.29) and George Henshaw (no.30), like flies to excrement, were inevitably drawn to lodgings in Knob Yard, Red Lion Street, Narrow Marsh. It seems they were not too keen on their digs: when apprehended the next evening, breaking into a private house on Station Street, they told the capturing officer they'd only gone there for a good night's sleep! Unfortunately the full details told another tale.

The arresting officer, P.C. Sanday, had actually witnessed the attempted break-in.

The policeman watched as a window was forced and Henshaw entered the premises. With both men now separated Sanday pounced, arresting Thompson and handcuffing him to the iron railings. He then seized Henshaw in the house. Neither man resisted, which was a good thing for the plucky Sanday, as one of the defendants was a 'pugilist' by profession.

Being 'bad characters' known to the police, Henshaw and Thompson were remanded for eight days before serving three months with hard labour.

Petty crimes were extensively reported in the local papers, with an almost conveyor-belt mentality at work in the editor's office. The following offences appeared under the headline **Only Borrowed**.

Ada Johnson [no. 38], charwoman, and Edwin Moorhouse [no. 39], labourer, of 4, Count-street, were charged with stealing sheets, pillowslips, and other articles of the value of £1, from Jessie Clinch, of 51, Sherwin Street. Prosecutrix had employed Johnson as charwoman, and on returning after a fortnight's holiday missed the property, which she found Moorhouse had offered in pledge at various shops. Prisoners pleaded guilty but at the same time the man said it was only a case of borrowing in an emergency. He had been convicted before and was given a month. Johnson had to pay 20s., or serve 14 days.

43. George Dykes was a fish freak. He was gaoled for seven days in 1896 for taking a tin of salmon and again in 1909 (14 days) for stealing a haddock.

DETAILS OF 50 PRISONERS WHO APPEARED BEFORE THE COURTS IN SPRING, 1908

(From the prison record books at Nottingham archives)

NAME	AGE	HEIGHT	JOB	ADDRESS	CHARGE	SENTENCE
1. George Brown	17	5' 4"	pit lad	40 Wycliffe St.	stealing 2s.6d.	probation
2. Susan Terry	39	4' 8"	lace-hand	1, Smith Yard	stealing shirt value 6s.6d	probation
3. John Beardsmore	35	5' 4"	lace-hand	Millstone La.	stealing a hatchet	fine 20s.
4. Robert Johnson	50	5' 5"	rag and bone gatherer	no residence	being on premises	1 month H.L.
5. James Smith	18	5' 4"	striker	5, Sherridan St.	stealing coal	14 days H.L.
6. George Smith	35	5' 6"	hawker	no fixed abode	loitering with intent	3 months H.L.
7. Daniel Foster	8	5' 10"	bookmaker's clerk	Liverpool	stealing case of silk	10 months H.L.
8. Leonard Searcey	18	5' 6"	labourer	15, Sherridan St.	stealing coal	14 days H.L.
9. Elizabeth Smart	18	5' 0"	shoe-hand	Riley's common lodging hse N.M.	stealing watch	2 months H.L.
10. John Woodward	18	5' 6"	milk seller	"	"	1 month H.L.
11. Leonard King	17	5' 1"	labourer	22, Byron St.	stealing brass name plate	not proceeded with
12. Elizabeth Lancaster	39	5' 3"	charwoman	Narrow Marsh	stealing counterpane	adj. gen.
13. Thomas Knight	45	5' 5"	labourer	Narrow Marsh	stealing pair of boots	14 days H.L.
14. Jacob Frost	24	5' 7"	pedlar	tramping	stealing a shirt	fine 20s.
15. Herbert Shipley	16	4' 4"	sells matches	Derby	stealing undervest	12 months probation
16. Alfred Tomlinson	18	5' 0"	"	"	"	"
17. Benjamin Cunningham	26	5' 6"	hawker	St John's Church Yard	stealing oil-cloth value 17s 6d	3 months H.L.
18. Fanny Graham	54	5' 3"	tailoress	53, Narrow Marsh	larceny from person	14 days H.L.
19. John Nightingale	23	5' 4"	labourer	13, Mount St Basford	stealing lace	adj. gen.
20. Robert Leverton	20	6' 0"	labourer	58, Kingston St	possessing house-breaking implements	discharged
21. George Farands	24	5' 5"	labourer	Windmill Lane	"	"
22. William Fletcher	54	5' 4"	bricklayer	31, Foster St. Radford`	stealing lead piping	adj. gen.
23. Percy Thompson	16	5' 3"	carter	262, High St. Basford	stealing a coat	not proceeded with
24. Martha Smith	45	5' 5"	charwoman	Dearing St.	stealing two pairs of boots	3 months H.L.

NAME	AGE	HEIGHT	JOB	ADDRESS	CHARGE	SENTENCE
25. Joseph Graham	74	5' 6"	pauper	Bagthorpe Workhouse	stealing pillow slip	discharged
26. Mildred Clarke	35	5' 4"	married	7, Temple Place	stealing two sheets, quilts, blankets	probation
27. William Annes	28	5' 5"	labourer	17, Windmill Lane	indecent exposure	probation (6 months)
28. William Dykes	34	5' 4"	porter	9, Denmark Court	assault	one month H.L.
29. Thomas Thompson	26	5' 6"	labourer/ pugilist	Lodging Houses	being on enclosed premises	3 months H.L.
30. George Henshaw	31	5' 6"	labourer	"	"	"
31. William Evans	23	5' 0"	labourer	"	stealing a box of fish (value 10s.)	3 months H.L.
32. Edward Woodcock	22	5' 6"	labourer	9, Machim St.	stealing watch and medals	probation
33. John Allcock	40	5' 8"	traveller	19, Wilford Grove	embezzlement	1 month H.L.
34. Raymond Trout	17	5' 5"	labourer	5, Royston Terrace	stealing bicycle lamp	7 days H.L.
35. John Murden	30	5' 6"	carter	Hawthorne St.	stealing three fowls	adj. gen.
36. Samuel Goller	23	5' 6"	hawker	1, Nat Yard	stealing programmes	1 month H.L.
37. Harold Chamberlain	21	5' 9"	hawker	15, Canal St.	vagrancy act	3 months H.L.
38. Ada Johnnson	51	5' 4"	charwoman	4, Count St.	stealing six sheets and pillow slips	fine 20s.
39. Edward Moorhouse	52	5' 2"	labourer	"	"	1 month H.L.
40. Elizabeth Wooward	26	5' 5"	laceworker	10, Knob Yard Narrow Marsh	larceny from person	14 days H.L.
41. Fanny Winters	24	4' 11"	"	"	"	"
42. Thomas Richardson	20	5' 6"	hawker	Bush's Lodging House, N.M.	stealing programmes	discharged
43. Richard Dixon	36	5' 1"	carter	41, Alderney St., Lenton	stealing coal	14 days H.L.
44. Thomas Goller	25	6' 2"	hawker	19, Mortimore St.	stealing programmes	discharged
45. Jack Matthews	23	5' 5"	labourer	174, Kirkewhite St.	warehouse breaking	adj. gen
46. Samuel Wilson	24	5' 8"	shoemaker	Lodging Houses	stealing metal watch	3 months H.L.
47. William Beech	50	5' 7"	chemist's assistant	no settled residence	loitering	3 months H.L.
48. Thomas Edge	34	5' 6"	labourer	Derby	being in possession	discharged
49. John Tyson	38	5' 9"	"	"	"	"
50. George Adams	20	5' 9"	labourer	no fixed abode	shopbreaking	6 months H.L.

H.L. = hard labour   ADJ. GEN. = case adjourned (often not proceeded with)

44. *Hawkers in the Market Square. Everybody was obliged to make a living as best they could. The man on the right appears to be selling toy birds and possibly potted plant holders. Anything and everything, including female flesh had its price at the market. Most crime in the Square was caused by drunken brawling, pickpocketing and disputes between customers and traders.*

Nos. (40) and (41), Elizabeth Woodward and Fanny Winters, were from the finishing school of petty criminals, Knob Yard, Narrow Marsh. Convicted of stealing a silver watch, a pipe and pouch and ten shillings from a Kimberley man, Frederick Warren, they were sent down for eight days.

Another inhabitant of Knob Yard was the fish fancier George Dykes. This master criminal progressed from lifting seafood from mongers' slabs to fishing in gentlemen's pockets for watches. Along with his accomplice, Samuel Wilson (no.46), Dykes served time (3 months) without a fish supper.

William Beech No (47) described himself as a chemists' assistant but professional dip would have been closer to the truth. He arrived fully equipped on an 'away-day' from London and did not bother to leave the station. When charged with loitering with intent Beech argued that he had only been looking for his boy. When searched he was found

to have a 'dummy' pocket in the left side of his jacket which enabled him to slip his hand out at the bottom in search of ill-gotten gains.

45. *Alice Dickinson convicted of stealing three shirts. Not the most interesting of offences but an excellent illustration of the fashions of the time. The courtroom appearance was enough to deter her from a life of crime, this being her only recorded offence.*

Alice Dickinson

40-86.

20-9-11

35

TALES FROM NOTTINGHAM'S PRISONS

BEFORE PENAL SERVITUDE

Before the days of lengthy sentencing, which began in the nineteenth century, other forms of punishment were meted out by church courts.

In 1569, Elizabeth Bate of St Mary's, Nottingham was in trouble for her custom of swearing many blasphemies contrary to the 34th injunction of the Queen. Pleading guilty, she was ordered to receive Holy Communion and to hear the curate read the homily against swearing.

In 1570, John Bradshawe of Nottingham was found guilty of committing bigamy with Katharine Burdocke and Joan Godbeheare. By today's standards his punishment seems bizarre:

The sayde Bradshawe shall go from the Parishe Churche of St Maryes this Saterdaye with a sheete about his myddell and a white wand in his hande after the manner of a penytent round about the markett place and a paper upon his backe which shall declare wherefore hee ys enjoined the pennunce and the said Katheryne Burdocke and Jane Godbeheare shall follow him in lyke manner.

In 1577 Henry Newton, an alderman, *committed fornication with one unknown in the fields* - he got off after swearing his innocence on the Bible!

Marital problems and incompatibility have been with us since time began. In 1617, Mr. Allen, speaking for Susanna Cawton, alleged that it was impossible for his client to live in the same house as her husband, James, without detriment to her health and risk to her life. He went on to argue that James used 'insulting words' and had *badly and inhumanely beaten Susanna and laid violent hands upon her and still detained her clothes or some of them, and withheld nourishment from her although due to her by law as his wife.*
James refused to pay the weekly two shillings maintenance ordered by the court and was duly excommunicated.

Other cases included charges for *hunting on the sabaoth daye*, for fighting in *Eveninge Prayer tyme* and *for keeping a house of bawdrie*. For the last offence, recorded in 1625, Edmund Garland was forced to do penance for three days *with capital letters on his brest and back.*

In the eighteenth and early nineteenth centuries thousands of offenders were transported, firstly to the United States and later to Australia. When the governments of these destinations refused to take any more prisoners the authorities were forced to accommodate their malefactors at home. Throughout the eighteen hundreds a massive prison building programme was undertaken to supplement and sometimes replace the inadequate gaols.

THE COUNTY GAOL IN 1872

A study of convictions in 1872 reveals that 88 people were detained for theft, 38 for assault and 25 on drink-related charges, In the County Gaol behind the Shire Hall other offences included: exposing an infant child so as to endanger life (at Bilborough); bastardy; attempt to rape; rape; bestiality; concealment of birth; threatening; damaging and carnage; being a tramp; being a deserter; being drunk on the highway (Phyllis Carter, age 63).

Articles stolen by those imprisoned for theft in the period 1870-72 include:-

17 duck eggs, 6 hen eggs, a fiddle, pigeon eggs, father's boots, beans, fruit, a horse, picture frame, mother's clothes, ducks, a dead hare, a pork pie, a shirt, tea-kettle, sheep, straw, a plaice, a hat, silver watch, umbrella, whip, wheelbarrow, fishing-rod, knives and forks, potatoes, a muff, shawl, pencil case, half a hundred weight of coal, bread, writing desk, turnips, cheese, 2 dead rabbits, an accordion, peas, strawberries, a pig's head, mole traps. (What, no cuddly toy?!)

Sentencing was very hit and miss. Young offenders were often given six strokes for offences such as stealing six duck eggs. The punishment for stealing a French poodle was one month's imprisonment. Hard labour might also be added to the sentence e.g. 7 days for stealing a pack of cards, Mary Darbyshire received 14 days for stealing three haddocks and George Whittington in 1898 one month for *indecent exposure with intent to insult females.*

46. Interior of the men's block in the House of Correction. It was almost certainly here that Dr. Alex McCook spent nine weeks in the winter of 1879, roughly the date of the photo. All prisoners were transferred to the new Bagthorpe Prison in 1891 as St John's was not big enough and conditions considered too harsh even by Victorian standards.

In 1900 two cases were brought before the magistrates on the same day and the same punishment deemed appropriate:-

William Wilkinson, a collier, sent his common-law wife Emma Moore to fetch some beer to their home at 19, Randall Street. Whether the ale wasn't to his taste or he felt that he had been waiting too long for it is not stated in the report. At all events, as soon as Emma stepped through the door Wilkinson pounced. He knocked her to the ground and set about her with both fists and feet, kicking her viciously in the face. He argued that Emma had been the aggressor, but the magistrates ruled against him, albeit adding they believed he was provoked.

He was ordered to pay a fine of 20 shillings or go to prison for 14 days.

In the same court, Catherine Monaghan was forced to make the same choice after being caught without a ticket on a train from Mansfield to Nottingham.

PRISONERS' TATTOOS

Both photographic and later, fingerprint records, were used to help in the identification of prisoners, many of whom had several aliases. Police also recorded distinguishing marks or features. Several of the prisoners sported tattoos. Aside from the usual assortment of 'I love Bill's' and 'true love's', these ranged from the still familiar self-inflicted dots on the back of the hand, to professionally administered ships in full rig sailing across the offender's chest. Others tattooed their initials - lest they forget - while the more circumspect inked in letters, for example, VSHH and IHAH, whose significance they alone knew. [Any suggestions?]

The following designs were noted on inmates at the turn of the century:

Woman's head and bust; woman's head and hat; women in tights; figure of female with 'you naughty flea' written over it; figure of nude female on globe; Japanese lady; a ballet girl; the Stars and Stripes; the Statue of Liberty; the Union Jack; three fish entwined on the left wrist; horse's head in a horseshoe; a snake charmer; a pigeon; a bear; a lizard; Buffalo Bill's head; a sailor dancing the hornpipe; flowers in a pot; a rose; a harp; a shamrock and a thistle.

In 1898 one 13-year-old prisoner was given six strokes for shoplifting.He had no chance of assuming a different identity. Arthur Percival spent most of his time with tattoo artists and as an older teenager sported the following gallery of images:

Tombstone; sailor and cross flags; V.R.; ship; sail; heart and anchor; bird; flower; soldier; woman; pigeon; bracelet and woman's head; star on back of hand; bear; woman; flower; cross flags; 'Florie'; ship; rose; love; 'Dear Florie and Horace' in wreath; Maltese cross; three dogs and ship, back of left hand; ring all left fingers; clasped hands on chest; dog, pigeon on left thigh; bracelet, left ankle; flower, calf left leg; full-rigged ship, elephant on diaphragm; snake, woman, left leg and thigh.

VICTORIAN PRISON LIFE

For much of the nineteenth century most offenders in Nottingham were confined for periods of days, months or years in cells in the St. John's Street House of Correction, the notorious Town Gaol or the County Gaol, Shire Hall. In 1891 all prisoners were transferred to the present prison, some 2-3 miles north of the city centre, then named Bagthorpe Gaol, after the area in which it was built. One of the earliest references to the site was in 1554 when it was known as *Buggerthorpe Felde.*

The older prisons were closed down because of what were, even by Victorian standards, atrocious and inhumane conditions. With the rapid influx of Victorian morals, the existing facilities were also much too small and without room for expansion. The situation called for purpose built establishments.

Prison reminiscences are fairly rare because most inmates were barely literate and their oral histories rarely recorded. Because of the stigma attached to being an ex-con those who could write often chose not to do so. The few who made it into print usually wrote under pseudonyms, e.g. "Ticket-of-leave-man" or "One-who-has-experienced-it."

Nottingham is fortunate in having a published edition of the first hand account of a Doctor who spent nine weeks on remand, almost certainly in St John's Street House of Correction. He was so affected by the dehumanising experiences he both witnessed and endured that he sought to share them with others. Dr. Alex McCook, a Scot, as his name suggests, was arrested in November 1879 for attacking his wife with a knife. Because of an extraordinarily high bail demand (£200) he had to await his trial in prison.

He was convinced of his innocence but as with all domestic disputes there were two sides to the story and his wife's testimony about the attack reveals a rather bizarre relationship. Her husband suffered from enormous mood swings; alternately threatening to kill her and then nursing her wounds following a frenzied attack:

47. The Chief Constable P.S. Clay takes delivery of a black Maria used to transport prisoners between the court and prison. This photo was taken in Shakespeare Street in 1895.

48. The main building of the St John's Street House of Correction was pulled down at the turn of the century.

I am the wife of the prisoner. I was married to him in 1876. I live in Arkwright Street. I went home on the afternoon of 27th (November) and found the defendant in his study...he went into the dining room and then said:

'A patient has insulted me. The English are all liars and thieves and I will have it out with you.'

He then rushed at me and seizing me by both my arms, he dragged me about the room. He gave me a blow upon the left jaw with his fist. He said during this time:

'I shall murder you I know I shall.'

He said this three times. We both then sat down again and went on with our tea. He then said:

'I shall make you and your friends regret you ever knew me.'

He then took up a small knife from the table and came towards me with the knife in his hand. I put out my left hand and got a blow upon it with the knife. My hand was cut and has been attended to. My husband was close to me and struck at me with the knife. He said:

'I shall have your life.'

I replied: 'I think that is enough; what shall I do?'

He said: 'Go and bathe it in cold water.'

Having plastered my hand up he gave me a blow upon the head which sent me reeling against a wall. I screamed as I had done when he was dragging me about.

I then went back to my tea. We sat down together and then he rushed me once more and gave me a kick as I was sitting down.

At the conclusion of this rather muddled testimony, and following the high demand for bail, Dr. McCook seemed resigned to his fate:

I will go to prison. Turning to his wife he added: Kiss the babies for me, love.

The atrocious conditions in the cells as related by an inmate

McCook was imprisoned in Nottingham one year after the Home Office took responsibility for all gaols in England in 1878. The prison regime would have varied little throughout the country. Let's hear a little of how McCook adapted to his new, spartan surroundings:

ADMISSION

There were about fifteen of us, male and female - a curious group when seen together. Arrived in the prison yard, which, in the town of _____ adjoins the police cells, we were marched into the prison vestibule, and ordered to stand in single file, and a little distance apart from each other, in the presence of the governor, who was there to receive and inspect us.

...I was thereupon conducted to a bathroom in the basement and was soon revelling in this well-timed luxury. But the bathroom was draughty and the toilet-ware very limited as was also the time allowed me. However, the dip, such as it was, proved delicious. It was also the only bath of the kind I had during my stay in prison. Having dressed again in the same unseasonable suit in which I was arrested, and which it was my lot to wear during the whole period of my incarceration - linens alone excepted - I was shown into a pretty comfortable cell on the basement with a boarded floor, and sorely did I regret my move therefrom.

...A warder entered my cell, which I had hardly time to inspect, and asked me civilly enough to follow him, which I did most willingly, not suspecting the nature of the change. We ascended several flights of iron stairs, which were polished painfully clean, and whose bannisters shone like a mirror. On reaching the top landing I followed him to the extreme end of a long corridor, where he halted, and, thrusting a key into the door, ushered me into a cell, remarking at the same time that if I wanted anything to ask the governor on his rounds. This cell was in marked contrast to the one I had just quitted, excepting in size. The floor was of huge stone slabs, and altogether it had a most cheerless and discouraging appearance. Moreover, I soon found out that it had a northern aspect, and was an outside cell. Scarcely had the warder taken his departure when I began to realise my terrible position, as well as the intensity of the cold. Want of sleep and of food, and the excitement of the day, increased my susceptibility, and I began to shiver beyond possibility of control. Never had I felt so cold in the course of my thirty-one years' existence, and so powerless to grapple with it. This was a true physiological cold, the demand for the necessary fuel having far exceeded the supply.

Seeing a much worn and well-patched rug lying in a corner of the cell, I grasped it as well as I could and threw it round my shoulders, and kept moving about to the best of my ability. How many degrees below the temperature of the one I had just left, I had no means of determining, but it must have been at least zero...

49. The awful conditions experienced in many prisons both before and after the Home Office assumed responsibility for all gaols in Britain in 1878. Most floggings were administered for attacks on warders, prisoners might receive twelve strokes with the cat. The treadmill was so fatiguing that many would deliberately maim themselves to try and avoid the daily grind.

41

FELLOW PRISONERS

What the deuce is this? Distant screams, mingled with heavy footsteps and banging of doors, first fell on my acute ears. Then followed horrid imprecations as the footsteps reached the top of the stair, and before I had time to fully realise the facts, a wretched Magdalene was deposited with a screech next door to me. The officers of the law departed with promptitude, and only too plainly showed their disgust by their zeal in closing the iron doors behind them, which caused the place to quiver and resound like a bombarded fort. But this was music to the melody next door.

That poor, fallen daughter of Eve yelled and shrieked, and blasphemed and vituperated against all humanity, and policemen in particular, for a full hour; still she swore and hissed like a very demon, till her drunken snore resounded throughout the echoing corridor, and peace, or quietness at least, at last being restored, I resumed my recumbency, determined to sleep. It was about two o'clock and my hopes ran high as I felt, once more, the sweet influence of Morpheus steal over me in response to the lullaby of snoring, drunken, degraded, outcast humanity....

CONVICTED PRISONERS

50. *The crank, like the treadmill, served no useful purpose whatsoever. In Nottingham this was the first task many prisoners had to undertake before breakfast.*

Being on remand Dr. McCook was allowed to wear his own clothes, and more importantly did not have to perform any of the futile, energy-sapping tasks of the convicted prisoner, although he could hear their groans throughout the day:

At nine o'clock the convicted prisoner resumes his labour, either in his cell, or out of doors; and in addition to my enforced idleness, I was obliged to listen to the horrid double "click" of the crank in a cell just above mine. From six to eight o'clock that "click" was incessant, and at nine it recommenced with the bell, and only ceased when the prisoner left his cell for exercise or devotions.

PRISON FOOD

Tea and supper duly arrived; a loud hand-bell proclaiming the cessation of labour, and the supper hour at a quarter to six.

Being at the extreme end of the corridor, I had time to mark the approach of the warders and their attendants, as door after door was rudely unlocked, and as rudely banged to again. My turn came at last, and the convict who acted as attendant to the warder in charge of my corridor, promptly placed a pint tinful of something, and a little dark brown loaf (six ounces) on my cell table, and immediately turned away with a broad grin on his face. Before closing the door, the warder directed my attention to a wooden spoon and a small wooden salt cellar on a slab in one corner of the cell. The tin and its contents were the first to receive my particular attention, for since breakfast at eight o'clock in the police cell, on my round of unbuttered bread and drink of inferior tea, my appetite had gained point. There stood the tin full to the brim of thick insipid water gruel, and the solitary little loaf of coarse brown bread by its side. To reduce this mess to palatable fare turned out to be an impossibility, for the addition of salt in anything like sufficient quantity, induced such intense thirst as to make swallowing painful. Sheer hunger and its attendant exhaustion forced me to swallow about half a dozen wooden spoonfuls, but beyond that I failed to go, in the presence of threatened vomiting.

Although it was mid-winter, on four out of the seven days - viz.,Sunday, Monday, Wednesday and Friday, the dinner was cold. The Sunday and Wednesday dinner of four ounces of bread and six of potatoes and suet pudding each, is especially to be condemned. The potatoes are served up in their jackets, and during the whole of my incarceration were scarcely fit to eat. They usually consisted of two, or occasionally three shabby-looking tubers, the dirt still adhering to them, and soft and spongy to the taste. One had got to use one's teeth or nails to divest them of their mother earth and their "jackets". As for the so-called suet pudding, it was as dry as a bone and tasteless, the bits of suet being always visible to the naked eye.

Being a doctor, McCook remarked on the malodorous and medical effects of the prison diet:

It induces an amount of painful flatulency and abdominal distention which adds much to the prisoner's misery...Nor is his flatulency merely an inconvenience. A prisoner can soon poison the limited column of air in his cell, and if not attentive to the ventilation, such as it is, he will soon find himself in a mephitic atmosphere...

Another consequence of this coarse and indigestible fare, is the production of piles, and violent local irritation. The prisoner is under constant mental strain, and is frequently convulsed with paroxysms of anguish, which reduce him to despair. Piles, forsooth, everybody has the piles!

At his trial nine weeks after admission, Dr. McCook was found not guilty and released. We can only hope that, with an improved diet, the Doctor's pain eased and that his taste of prison life curbed his Celtic temper.

BRUTAL MURDER AT BAGTHORPE GAOL

In 1930 the role of Bagthorpe was changed from that of a main line gaol to a young adult offender's prison, in which a regime of harsh discipline was imposed on delinquent youths.

Prisoners rose at 6.00.a.m. every day and were forced to exercise until breakfast 85 minutes later. Work began at 8.a.m. and was a twelve hour shift with breaks of one hour for lunch and forty minutes for tea. Nobody could accuse the prison authorities of being profligate with taxpayer's money: prisoners worked in fields and gardens around the prison and were only paid after working 29 hours. The rate for enforced labour was a princely one half-penny per hour. At 8.p.m., the end of the working day, prisoners were allowed to associate, smoke and play games for thirty minutes before lights out.

The prison became a borstal in 1932 and by 1940 had changed to a borstal recall centre, where young offenders who broke the terms of their release were recalled to serve out their full sentences. By the end of the Second World War, Sherwood Borstal had the unenviable reputation of being one of the roughest, toughest and strictest centres of its kind in Britain. It housed thugs and bullies, barons and wide-boys and attacks upon staff with hammers, axes, iron bars and chairs were commonplace.

Matters were brought to a tragic head on November 19th 1948. Kenneth Strickson used to help in the cleaning of the prison chapel. Since his father's suicide, Strickson had spent most of his life in institutions. He needed love, care and attention but did not know how to set about getting them. One day the 21-year-old found himself alone in the chapel with the 46-year-old matron, Irene May. She was bending over, cleaning, and Strickson made an indecent suggestion. Instead of reporting the proposal the matron simply replied:

It's a good job I'm broad-minded.

Whether the offender took this as a come-on or not is unsure. The next day he confided to a fellow prisoner:

I am going to the chapel with the matron. I am going to have a go at her up there. I am going to see what I can get out of her.

With his sexual advances being spurned by the matron the frustrated young man flew into an uncontrollable tantrum, unmercifully battering the poor unsuspecting woman about the head so ferociously that the legs of two chairs broke clean off. Irene's head was described as having been 'beaten to shreds', with fragments of skull embedded in the brain.

Strickson stole the dead woman's keys, locked the door to the chapel and tried to join an outside team of workers and bluff his way out of prison. When his ploy failed, he made his way to the chief's office and confessed:

Will you go to the chapel, sir? I have killed the matron.

Kenneth Strickson was hanged at Lincoln Prison. The ghost of the matron, Mrs. Irene May Phillips, is still said to haunt the chapel.

'TAKING A DRINK AND ASSAULTING A SERGEANT'

THE BOBBY'S SHELTER; OR, A BRIGHT SPOT ON A NIGHT BEAT.

51. The policeman often had his own interpretation of community policing. The Victorian bobby was told that he should be 'bold in action'. Well, he was just obeying orders.

Misdemeanours by the boys in blue and a look at the lighter side of criminal life

The policeman's lot in Nottingham was not (always) a happy one. They were expected to be *bold in action, have a perfect command of temper, keep their boots and belts polished and never to carry an umbrella on duty.*

Discipline was enforced with a range of punishments from fines to dismissal. Details from the police punishment book covering the period from 1870-1920 reveal a whole range of offences including:-

1). Being asleep when on duty
2). Being found asleep in a cab shelter
3). Frequenting public houses
4). Being in a brewery
5). Gossiping while on duty (fine 5 shillings)
6). Gossiping and smoking
7). Being absent without leave
8). Using unsuitable language to a superior officer
9). Assaulting D.S.Clark (fine 5 shillings)
10). Taking a drink and assaulting a sergeant
11). Allowing a prisoner to escape (fine 10 shillings)
12). Removing a dead body without instructions (fine 7s.6d.)
13). Not finding a pawnshop door insecure
14). Taking home a bugle taken from some boys
15). Improper conduct in making untruthful statements in a police report
16). Showing a want of intelligence in the execution of duty
17). Not using sufficient energy to arrest 3 men suspected of larceny
18). Being off beat and in a house of supposed ill repute (dismissal)
19). Indecent behaviour to Douglas Pyatt aged 14 years (dismissal)
20). Sexual intercourse with a married woman
21). Improper relations with a German's wife

We can all sleep safely in our beds knowing that today's policemen and women, respected by us all, would never contemplate committing any of the above offences.

THE LIGHTER SIDE OF COURT LIFE

There was much to mock in the hypocritical attitudes of Nottingham folk in Victorian times. Two papers, *The Jackdaw* and *The Owl*, adopted a tongue-in-cheek style when reporting from the courtroom. The following extracts are from both papers, 1878-9:

Mr. Thomas Torr, of Basford, was always of weak intellect, and has been weak enough to die since Mr. Charles Groves, ale and porter merchant, *drove over the unfortunate fellow with a horse and trap — so much the worse for imbeciles! Can the great business of the world be impeded to save their silly bacon?*

Samuel Bates has come to the police court once more. His former appearances were for the unwarrantable offence of wife-beating. From a public point of view, however, the offence for which Bates last stood in the dock was more unwarrantable. He had been found guilty of adulterating milk with water, to the audacious extent of 30 per cent.

52. *The hallelujah sisters of the Salvation Army. Meetings and marches met with mixed receptions amongst the local population.*

Alfred, the Bulwell carter, envious of the notoriety of Councillor Holmes, got drunk on Good Friday and amused himself by smashing his father's lamps and ornaments and chasing his sister with a naked knife. The dear boy has been in the habit of getting delightfully drunk two or three times every week, and it will go very hard with him to be shut up a month in gaol without his usual fun and allowances.

The editors took particular exception to the Sunday meetings and marches of the newly formed Salvation Army and implied that many were solely interested in making money:

We cannot get away from the fact the beginning and the middle and the end of all these demonstrations is first the nobbing box, second the nobbing box, and for the third and last time the nobbing box.

The following snippet is taken from *The Jackdaw* in 1879, with once again the target being the Salvation Army at Sneinton Market. It went out under the following headline

The Hallelujah Sisters in Nottingham:

The day being very dull I thought I would follow the "Army", and witness the promised overthrow of Satan and rout of his imps. The leading brothers formed themselves in a row, arm-in-arm, preceded by two or three of the leading sisters, walking backwards, who led the others in singing hymns, and beating time with their umbrellas... one of the leading sisters called upon a middle aged person in black to give her experiences of the benefits she had received from enlisting in the Salvation Army...She commenced by stating that 18 months ago she was one of the biggest infidels, and now 'I stand here as a monument of God's mercy, I have been an infidel for 25 years'. At this part, a young woman, in a seat next to me, kept interrupting the proceedings, exclaiming what a sinner she was, seeming in great distress. Whether her feelings were touched by the Gospel, or by alcoholic stimulants, I could not decide...there was frequent shouting and continued hallelujahs from an individual well known to the Sneintonians as 'Jumping Jack'.

53. Police on parade in the Market Square in 1898.

46

THE DISGRACE OF A NOTTINGHAM PREACHER

The trial of John Jackson; preacher, mesmerist and attempted rapist.

INDECENT ASSAULT•CASE – NOTTINGHAM.

JOHN JACKSON – FROM A PHOTO

54. John Jackson used hypnotism, drugs, prayer and brute force in his attempted rapes of young believers.

The face of religion was not always so innocent.

In April 1882, a 25-year-old Nottingham woman was the first to give testimony in an allegation of attempted rape. A 38-year-old man in the dock with a heavy, apostolic beard, listened intently as a succession of young women followed. The prisoner was John Jackson, a minister of the 'Gospel Band' Chapel, Blue Bell Hill. Over a period of years he had been enticing female members of his religious group back to his Sneinton home. There, by the combined use of religion, mesmerism, drugs and sheer brute force he afflicted serious sexual assaults upon the unsuspecting believers. Once the first victim had the courage to bring charges, a succession of further victims appeared, all complaining of the deranged minister's offensive behaviour.

Their stories revealed a consistent *modus operandi*. The first distressed victim gave the following evidence relating to events which occurred at the defendant's private rooms, South Street, Sneinton:

I called about seven o'clock in the evening. I knocked at the door and the prisoner opened it. I asked him about the banner when I got inside. He was sitting on the other side of the table. He talked about the banner and said it had been bought, and he showed me the inscription that was to be placed on it. He then began to talk to me about young men, and kept his eyes firmly fixed on my face. He wanted to know if I went with any young man in the band, and I said 'no'. He then said something about how soon young men ruined girls and I got up, not approving of his manner.

I went towards the door when the prisoner threw me on the couch. He put one hand over my mouth, and attempted to commit an assault upon me. I struggled to get away from him, but I could not. We rolled on the floor together and he again tried to commit an offence....The door was ultimately unfastened by the prisoner. Before he did so he prayed for me, and talked about the woman taken in adultery recorded in the Bible. He knelt down and thanked God that he could keep a girl pure and virtuous.

A 21-year-old from Storer Street, also invited to the prisoner's home, was the second to give evidence:

I sat on the sofa and he stood over me wafting his hands about my face. Not producing any effect upon me, he went to the cupboard and put something on his handkerchief and returned. He wafted the handkerchief about my face, and I became unconscious. When I became conscious I found that he was placing his hands about my body in an indecent manner. I asked him what he was doing, and told him that I had not come to be insulted...He got hold of my hand and acted indecently. I asked him to let me out and he said: 'I have already ruined you in the eyes of your brother and you must let me do what I want.' I asked him what he had done it for and he said: 'Because I love you, and have loved you for a long time.'

I told him that he had no right to talk like that to me. He said: 'What do you know? You are only a child, and don't you think I know better than you? You have no right to dictate to me.'

He said he would let me go if I would promise to come again. I promised to go again and not tell anyone what he had said and done. I did not mean to go again. I was willing to promise anything to get away. He said: 'Let us pray,' and I said I could not. He said women did not know right from wrong and he knelt down and began to pray. He prayed that I might be made a pure young woman, and that my eyes might be opened to see that what he was doing was right and for my good. After that he let me out.

A third girl, only seventeen, told a similar story: questions about young men, an attempt to render her unconscious, fumbling, a prayer of forgiveness, promises not to tell, the unbolting of the door.

There was little the defence could do. Mr. Harris, acting for Jackson, said that his client was not on trial for immorality and implied that the victims may have consented. The jury disagreed and after just ten minutes deliberation returned a verdict of guilty on all counts. The Judge took great exception to the preacher's betrayal of his position:

I have sentenced many men standing where you now stand, some of them for crimes liable to more severe punishment than yours, but a viler wretch than you hardly ever stood in the dock.

Under the pretence of religion you had the baseness to attempt the virtue of a succession of young girls. You tried to ravage one of them, you tried to corrupt most of the others; and after you had done that which your filthy lust suggested to you, you had the disgusting blasphemy to fall on your knees and pray to God Almighty to keep them pure. I never, as I say, met with a more infamous wretch, and the infamy which will cling about you for the rest of your life will be at any rate not more than you deserve. I shall pass upon you sentence which the law will allow. It is not adequate to the crimes you have committed, but it is at all events one which will leave its mark upon you for the rest of your degraded existence.

The prisoner was visibly shaken at the sentence of two years hard labour - time enough to contemplate his twisted religious self-justifications.

Many women did not attend chapel but worshipped Bacchus instead.

55.

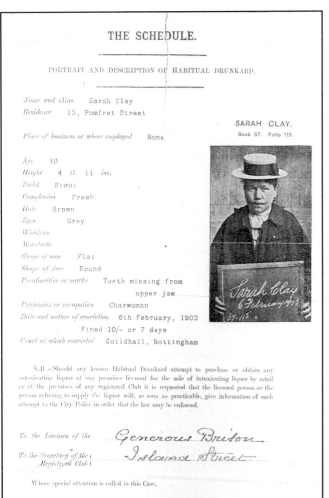

56.

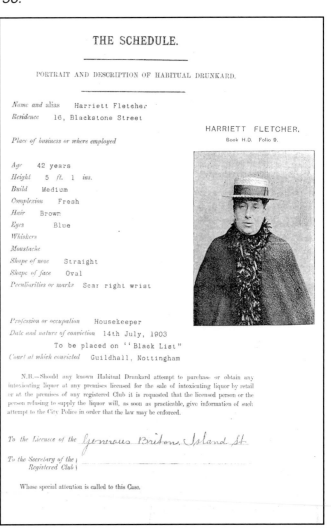

THE SCHEDULE.

PORTRAIT AND DESCRIPTION OF HABITUAL DRUNKARD.

Name and alias   Agnes Butler

Residence   7, Normanton Place,

         Normanton Street

Place of business or where employed   None

AGNES BUTLER.
Book H.D.   Folio 5.

Age   39

Height   5 ft. $1\frac{1}{4}$ ins.

Build   Slim

Complexion   Fresh

Hair   Dark Brown

Eyes   Grey

Whiskers

Moustache

Shape of nose   slightly bent

Shape of face   Oval

Peculiarities or marks Scar on right cheek bone,
    scar between eyes, scar right eye-brow

Profession or occupation   Married

Date and nature of conviction   9th March, 1903

         Fined 10/- or 7 days

Court at which convicted   Guildhall, Nottingham

N.B.—Should any known Habitual Drunkard attempt to purchase or obtain any intoxicating liquor at any premises licensed for the sale of intoxicating liquor by retail or at the premises of any registered Club it is requested that the licensed person or the person refusing to supply the liquor will, as soon as practicable, give information of such attempt to the City Police in order that the law may be enforced.

To the Licensee of the   *Generous Briton*

To the Secretary of the ⎰
        Registered Club ⎱ _____

Whose special attention is called to this Case.

57.

55-57. In an attempt to deal with the high incidence of public drunkenness the 'Habitual Drunkards Licensing Act' was introduced in 1902. Posters of habitual offenders were sent to pubs - in this case 'The Generous Briton'. If the offenders purchased, or tried to purchase, alcoholic liquor, within three years of their date of conviction, they were liable to an initial fine of 20 shillings rising to 40 shillings for subsequent offences.

    If the publican was found to be supplying the offenders with such liquor he was liable to a fine not exceeding £10 for the first offence and £20 for subsequent offences.

    The well-intentioned law had little chance of success given the high number of heavy drinkers.

THE OLDEST PROFESSION

58. *Another view of the Market Square c.1904. At night In the 1860's it was difficult to avoid being propositioned in the city centre by one of the 'degraded, wretched, drunken female hyenas' also known as prostitutes.*

'Drinking and debauching go on until any hour of the morning.'

If local newspaper reports are to be believed it was hard not to walk more than a hundred yards in the centre of Nottingham in the 1860's without being propositioned by a whore. These were described as *girls from the age of seventeen upwards, all tricked out in tawdry finery and looking to the letter the degraded things they had become.* Indeed, local reporters who visited the brothels - purely in a professional capacity of course! - were not sparing in their descriptions of prostitutes and their customers alike. The men were variously referred to as being *half drunk and stupid; disreputable; thieves; the early victims of parental neglect; old in depravity; brutalized and filthy.* The women were: *degraded; wretched; coarse; pitiable; abused; female Hyena; a brutal specimen of female culture; a female brute; debauched and reeling drunk.*

Parliament Street, Wheatsheaf Yard and Bellfounder's Lane were each home to several of the estimated fifty Nottingham brothels. These ranged from converted slum dwellings, to cheap coffee houses and well furnished establishments with erotic French prints on the wall to further arouse the customers.

Many brothels masqueraded under the names of working men's clubs and were therefore outside the normal licensing laws. Members paid an annual subscription of just 2s. 6d. and could legally enter their clubs after hours. In the chief constable's report of 1877 he derided them as:

...nothing more than places of resort, when the licensed houses are closed, where drinking and debauching go on until any hour of the morning, to the ruin of the individuals frequenting them, and, what is worse, of their wretched families.

Some of the most base establishments were in Bell Yard, their secrets being told in the book **Revelations of Nottingham Life**,

Here congregate the lowest, the vilest, and most debased of the profligate of Nottingham; round these fires of hells upon earth, called homes, may be seen clustered from eight to ten, or fourteen, persons of both sexes carousing, and openly indulging in the most shameless acts of indecency; the girls on the knees of their paramours, some far gone in intoxication, and all using language that is a disgrace to the sex, and falls like a blight upon the ear.

A nearby brothel was visited by reporters at 1.45.a.m.

On a low stool by a scanty remnant of fire sat a woman, described as the mistress of the house, busily employed in smoking: near her was the "bully" of the establishment - drunk, and swearing terribly; the dress had been torn in shreds from her person by the cowardly miscreant who had just left off beating her as the police arrived, and the poor infatuated wretch dared not give him in charge for fear of worse treatment another time.

On a dilapidated sofa in the same den, sat three girls with two men between them. The apartments were each about 16 feet square, and an air of squalid wretchedness pervaded the whole.

Possibly the most famous street walker of this time was 'Bostol Jane' who came to work as a domestic servant from her home town of Bostol in Leicestershire. Like thousands of other servants, she was seduced by her employer and spent the next twenty-two years walking her regular beat as a prostitute on Parliament Street. She was in every sense an old pro and highly respected by customers and fellow workers. She died at the age of fifty-one and the funeral chapel consequently witnessed it's largest assembly for decades, with the congregation including many young girls for whom she had become a mother figure. Throughout the funeral the rain lashed down with a ferocity that had not been seen in years, but once the coffin was completely covered the skies cleared and the wind abated. In those superstitious times many interpreted this as a judgment on her life.

59. Kate Handley seems to show little fear of the camera. She was another prostitute who assaulted her drunken punters.

Name _Ethel Yarnold._

AND

Aliases _Cissie Taylor._

Description.

Born at	_Worcester._
Trade or Calling	_Prostitute._
Age	_21 years._
Height	_5ft. 0in._
Build	_Proportionate._
Eyes	_Grey._
Complexion	_Fresh._
Hair	_Dark brown._
Beard	
Moustache	

Marks or Peculiarities _Small mole rt. cheek, bad front teeth._

60. The police details reveal all.

JUDGE FOUND IN A BROTHEL

In 1884 Mr. Justice Watkin Williams, a judge noted for his stance on immorality and vice was on circuit in Nottingham. Like so many respectable lawmakers and upholders of the nation's morals he did not always practice what he preached. The 56-year-old suffered a fatal heart attack whilst reaching a climax in one of the local brothels. His body was dumped outside the house in Foreman Street and he was eventually pronounced dead by a doctor. Two of his friends covertly collected him, transported his body back to his lodgings and tucked him up for the night. A second doctor was summoned and the newspapers were led to believe that the good judge had passed away in his lodgings. He received a glowing obituary from *The Times.*

The people of Nottingham, however, knew better, as the following memorial card demonstrates:

IN MEMORY OF

MR. JUSTICE WATKIN WILLIAMS

WHO DEPARTED THIS LIFE SUDDENLY AT

MRS. SALMANDS, NOTTINGHAM

THURSDAY NIGHT, JULY 17TH 1884

AGED 56 YEARS

IN EIGHT FEET DEEP OF SOLID EARTH

SIR WATKIN WILLIAMS LIES

HE LOST HIS BREATH, WHICH CAUSED HIS

DEATH

'TWIXT NELLY BLANKEY'S THIGHS.

SUFFER THE LITTLE CHILDREN

Abortion and the shocking cruelty shown to the city's youngest citizens

With no readily available, foolproof means of birth control, even as recently as the 1960's, there was a constant demand for the backstreet abortionist. At the turn of the century women seeking abortions fell into two broad categories: some, having already given birth to nine or ten children, were so worn out by the struggle to feed and clothe them they wanted no more. Others, especially domestic servants, would have lost their jobs once the pregnancies showed. Moreover pregnant, unmarried women were much frowned upon and usually ostracised from their community.

Some women gave birth secretly and either killed their babies immediately or abandoned them on doorsteps miles away. Contemporary newspapers make no great fuss over the discovery of dead babies, with details routinely reported. In 1882 a gardener informed the police that he had found the dead body of a female child in The Park. So common was the offence that the story merited only a couple of short, impersonal, matter-of-fact paragraphs in that day's paper:

The body, which was not covered up at all, appeared to have been dropped over the fence next to the Park, and there did not appear to have been any signs of concealment...

The anonymous infant was discovered lying on a piece of clothing, there were no visible marks of violence. At the inquest it was stated that the baby had breathed but *had not taken full inspiration -* she probably died a few seconds after birth. The cause of death was cited as *want of proper attention.*

TRAGEDY IN ARNOLD

Most women seeking to abort either acted alone or went to abortionists (mostly women) who were supposed to know about such matters: some did, some didn't! One of the second category was Elizabeth Topham who, on July 17th 1901, stood trial for her life following a botched termination. Alongside the 49-year-old barmaid stood her co-defendant, a mousy, simple-looking 34-year-old fish-dealer, Annie Benson, charged with being an accessory to murder.

Annie's main role in the tragic story was that of go-between: she introduced her friend, Louisa Allcock to Elizabeth Topham, a barmaid who supplemented her income as a backstreet abortionist. At 43, and already the mother of six

children, Louisa could take no more. Her husband's wages, those of a tanner's labourer, were barely enough to feed the family and the Allcocks really struggled to find the rent for their home in Westwood Road, Sneinton.

The fatal meeting took place on 10th June at 8.30.p.m. in the Old Volunteer pub in Carlton where Mrs. Topham had been working on and off as a barmaid for twelve months. After a brief discussion both women disappeared into the backyard which opened onto the street. The "operation" was carried out with some "instruments" brought from the prisoner's home, and lasted a mere ten minutes.

Louisa managed to limp home but the next evening her husband returned from work to find her seriously ill. She was visited in turn by Mrs. Topham, a midwife, a doctor and finally, one week later, by the police - the latter called in as her condition worsened. The wretched woman gave her deposition shortly before dying on 20th June.

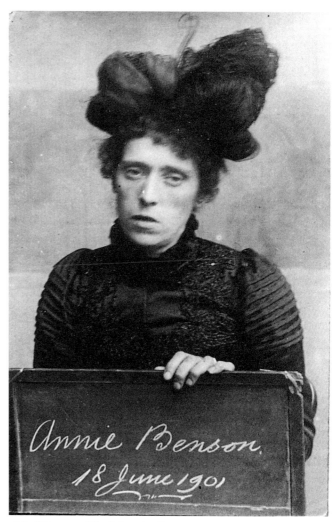

61. The terrified Annie Benson who introduced her friend Loisa Allcock to an abortionist...with tragic results.

At first Mrs. Topham denied ever having met Louisa, a defence adopted by the hapless Annie Benson. The latter, however, finally cracked under the pressure of police questioning and pointed the finger at the bloated barmaid.

At the ensuing trial the jury heard that Louisa had died from blood-poisoning doubtless caused by one or other of the tools of Mrs. Topham's gruesome trade. In her deposition Louisa Allcock stated she had been "operated" on by a woman whose name she did not know. The woman, Louisa stated, *carried ale* at the Volunteer Inn. Mrs. Benson's case was helped considerably by Louisa's confirmation that she had asked her to accompany her to the pub. The judge directed that as there was no evidence against Annie Benson, she should be discharged.

In his summing up, His Worship advised the jury that if they believed death was proved to have resulted from germs introduced by the "operation" it was their duty to find the prisoner guilty. They were out for just eight minutes.

The courtroom was hushed in anticipation when the jury returned. Elizabeth Topham clenched the front rail tightly with both hands, her knuckles white. The foreman stood to give the verdict:

We find the prisoner guilty but strongly recommend her to mercy.

Elizabeth's eyes began streaming tears as she collapsed into the arms of the two hard-faced female warders behind her. Turning her head towards heaven she prayed for forgiveness:

Oh, Lord help me; have mercy on me; Lord have mercy on me.

The judge was now at liberty to tell the jury that the prisoner had already served seven years for a similar offence. Donning the black cap he told the packed courtroom that he had no alternative but to pronounce the death penalty.

Elizabeth's friends sobbed and spoke quietly amongst themselves as she was helped from the court. Desperate for friendly human contact she managed to kiss and hug one or two, who stood close by, before being taken down to await execution.

The Lord did have mercy upon her as the sentence was eventually commuted to penal servitude for life.

BURTON ROAD.

62. The 'Old Volunteer' on Burton Road, Carlton. The botched abortion was carried out in the back yard.

63. Elizabeth Topham sentenced to death for a botched abortion in Carlton which was performed in ten minutes with a gruesome array of instruments. The 'operation' was directly responsible for the death of Louisa Allcock, a mother of six who died a few days later.

HOOPER'S PILLS AND EPSOM SALTS

Despite the expansion of Dr. Marie Stopes' family planning advice service in the twenties and thirties, large numbers of women still had unwanted pregnancies terminated. One such woman, who wished to remain anonymous, worked as a waitress at the Elite at this time. With her husband, a miner, being unemployed, she was the sole breadwinner. The couple couldn't afford replacement contraceptives and the male partner used to wash out and re-chalk the same tired French letter. Not surprisingly the woman 'fell' again. With pregnancy meaning dismissal for waitresses, she asked around as to how to induce an abortion. The methods recommended by 'knowing' women included: swallowing large quantities of Dr. Hoopers' pills or Epsom salts; putting your feet in hot mustard water; falling down the stairs; travelling on a bus; drinking a bottle of gin.

The anonymous waitress succeeded in her quest by using a silver spoon and Lysol. In her consequent stay in hospital, despite persistent questioning by doctors, she repeatedly denied that the pregnancy had been interfered with. Another woman, born in 1907, speaks of the same methods of aborting and also remembers another product, slippery elm, which was used as a pessary. Despite the double insurance of sponge and French letters the woman, who worked at Raleigh, still fell pregnant several times after she had completed her desired family of three. She used a variety of methods to 'lose' the other babies and recommended a woman in Radford whose main tool was a crochet hook.

Equally as sad as the crude cases of self-induced abortions were the stories of cruelty and neglect to young children.

Throughout the nineteenth and early twentieth centuries' the infant mortality rate in industrial areas was extremely high. Of every 1,000 children born in Nottingham in 1882, 188 never reached their first birthday. Of these, some would be killed by their mothers at birth. Proving infanticide was difficult and one must wonder how many deaths in the chart (p59), were accidental and how many were deliberate.

A typical problem facing the authorities was reported in the local press June, 1908:

STRANGE NOTTINGHAM CASE - CHILD DROWNED IN A BOWL

Extraordinary circumstances were brought to light at an inquest at the Hyson Green Coroner's Court, Nottingham, last evening. The case was that of the newly-born male infant of Eliza Wardle, a widow, living at 18, Smith-street, Denison-street.

Mary Barnes, registered midwife, of 86, Independent Street, spoke to being called to the house and to finding the child lying in a three-gallon tin bowl, which was full of water. Life was extinct. Witness made inquiries, and was told that the infant had been born into the bowl. She took the child out and laid it on the sofa.

Sara Outram, the landlady, said that when the birth took place she ran for a neighbour, and Mrs. Barnes was summoned. Witness stood at the door waiting for her, and when she went back into the room the child was in the bowl. There was little, if any, water in the bowl before the birth took place.

Dr. Allen's evidence showed that the body weighed 4lb. 11oz. and was fully developed. The child had had a separate existence, the lungs being fully expanded, and death was due to drowning.

The coroner remarked that he hardly thought they would be justified in closing the case without giving the mother a chance to give evidence.

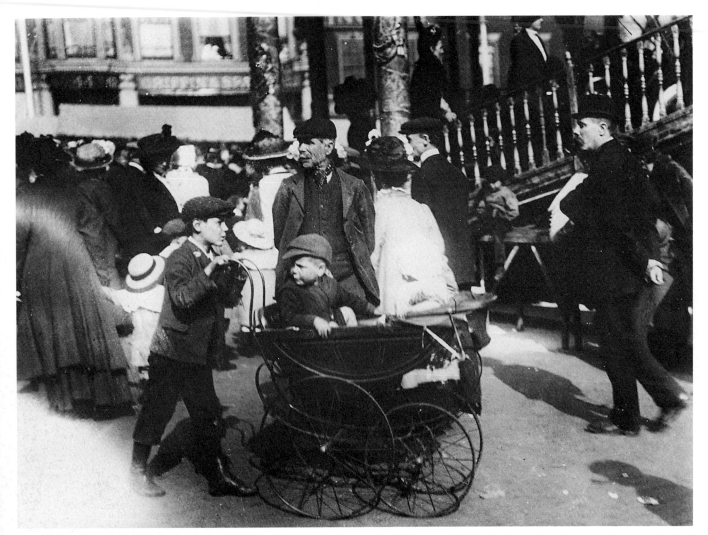

64. Children were often exploited by the criminal elements. They would train them to steal or beg and pass the proceeds on for fencing.

MOTHER PREFERS THE BOTTLE TO HER BABY

Some children were abandoned at birth, others fell prey to a gamut of illnesses caused by the atrocious living conditions in areas like Narrow Marsh and St Ann's. Occasionally, when the mother took to the bottle, the baby was neglected and simply starved to death. In December 1896, Elizabeth Lock, 30, from Bobber's Mill, stood before the court charged with the manslaughter of her eight-month-old son, Jonathan. No allegations of active violence towards the child were presented. The prosecution argued that the mother was responsible for her son's premature death due to her *not providing proper food and attention*.

Jonathan was the youngest of five children. The eldest, Bertha, aged 11, was often left to look after the younger members of the family whilst her mother was away all day. On one occasion she disappeared for three weeks and her children were cared for by a neighbour, Mrs. Moorhouse. She found the youngest child very dirty and when the mother disappeared again, this time for ten days, she determined to call in the doctor, who confirmed that Jonathan was suffering from insufficient nutrition. Put simply, the child was starving to death. Elizabeth returned to the family home on a Sunday in October and said she did not have enough money for food for the baby as she had spent it all on drink. The baby was left to lie on the sofa because the cradle had been chopped up to use for firewood. By Wednesday, Jonathan Lock, aged eight months, was found to be dead.

When charged with manslaughter Elizabeth simply asked:

How much time shall I get?

Bertha gave evidence against her mother who, she said, never went out to work, only to drink, always on Saturdays, Sundays, Mondays, Tuesdays and Wednesdays. The judge, determined to find out the truth about the prisoner's intemperance, questioned one of the defence witnesses, Mrs. Woodley, as follows:

JUDGE: *Do you keep a public-house?*
WITNESS: *No, sir, I sell herb beer.* (Laughter)
JUDGE: *Was the prisoner a customer of yours?*
WITNESS: *She sometimes had a few bottles.*
JUDGE: *She was a considerable consumer?*
WITNESS: *It is made of pure herbs, sir.* (Laughter)
JUDGE: *Oh, yes, I know, but she was a considerable consumer of this anti-alcoholic beverage?*
WITNESS: *She used to occasionally come for some.*

65. Children from Narrow Marsh shortly after WW1. Whole families would live in a single room and the overcrowded slum conditions were responsible for the high incidence of contagious diseases.

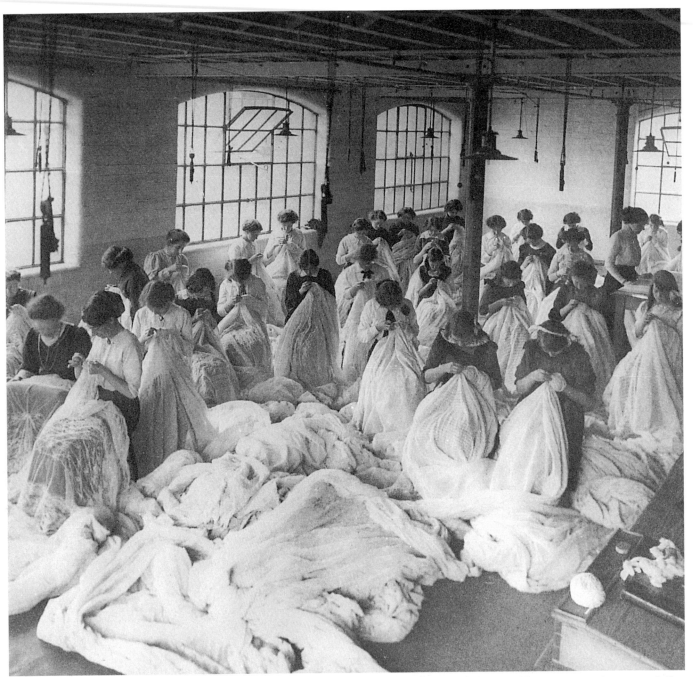

66-67. *The lace mills were amongst the major employers of female labour. Hours were long and the variations in temperature and poor working conditions were the cause of many health problems. A thermometer put on one girl's knee recorded a temperature of 148 degrees f. The girls showed a preference for tea and slops rather than solid food. In the 1860's sore throats and coughs were commonplace and many girls had their throats 'wrapped around'. Sickness, headaches, rheumatism and fainting fits due to the intense heat were accepted as being part of the job. Girls between 17 and 24 were particularly susceptible to tuberculosis.*

Elizabeth, contesting the medical evidence, argued that Jonathan had died from a convulsive fit. She further stated that she had fed the baby with condensed milk and that her husband did not provide her with enough money to pay doctor's fees. She said she would never have taken to the drink if her husband had not repeatedly abused her, regularly greeting her with the hard end of his boot when arriving home from work. Elizabeth argued that she had done her duty to the baby, that she had done all she could. The jury disagreed and pronounced her guilty as charged. On passing sentence, the Judge said the prisoner was well known as a drunken woman in the town and he thought it right to mark the grievous nature of the offence by sentencing her to eighteen months' hard labour.

Dr. Milner, working at Leen Side Mortuary in 1908, was shocked by the cases of death through emaciation due to lack of food. At the inquest of one of the many child fatalities, where a baby died of *convulsions,* he told the court that death through starvation was regarded as normal in the poorer inner-city areas and people did not bother much about it. He added that a baby's health was further impaired by the absence of fresh air and sunlight and the insanitary surroundings.

SOME CAUSES OF CHILD DEATHS IN NOTTINGHAM 1898/9

NAME	AGE	CAUSE OF DEATH
Pamela Beardsley	5	Burns accidentally caused.
Hilda Beardsmore	2	Burns but no evidence as to how originated.
Stephen Turpin	14mths	Accidentally suffocated.
Brown (male child)	-	Suffocation due to want of attention at birth.
Ward (female child)	-	Convulsions due to premature birth.
Daisy Brewster	9wks	Suffocated by vomit in air passages.
Ada Bagshaw	2	Accidentally overthrown from mail cart.
Ernest Taylor	5wks	*Felo de se*, by taking drugs to procure abortion.
Percy White	2	Rupture of blood vessel caused by fall.
George Dykes	5mths	Overdose of laudanum - misadventure.
Clara Rogers	4mths	Suffocated in bed with mother.
Ben Holmes	12wks	Bagthorpe Prison - malnutrition - manslaughter.
William Gibson	3mths	Suffocation while in bed with mother.
Albert Dean	3mths	Suffocation while in bed with mother.
Hubert Gardner	5days	Suffocation while in bed with mother.
Wright (male child)	-	Want of attention at birth.
Joseph Green	4mths	Suffocated while in bed with parents.
Elizabeth Forman	6	Suffocated while in bed with parents.
Varney Allsop	5mths	Malnutrition due to improper feeding.
Pritchett (male child)	5days	Malnutrition accelerated by exposure.
Unknown male child	-	Found dead - no evidence as to cause.
George Johns	4	Found drowned.
Dodd (male child)	-	Want of attention at birth.
Unknown (female child)	-	Found dead - want of attention at birth.
Ellen Edwards	6wks	Suffocation in bed with parents and two children.
Ada Brown	2	Accidentally drowned in a dolly tub.
George Dunraven	3wks	Misadventure - overdose of laudanum.

One can imagine the horror of waking up to find that you had laid on your child and caused death through suffocation. The likeliehood is high that not all such cases were accidents.

LACE JOINERS NOTTINGHAM

'OVERCROWDING, INTEMPERANCE AND BESTIAL FILTHINESS'

68. Every city has its seedy side. In Nottingham Narrow Marsh was synonymous with dirt and depravity. It became a Mecca for low life from all parts of the county who found accommodation in the cheap lodging houses. As today, alcohol led to many altercations, and there were no holds barred.

Life and death on Narrow Marsh - the worst slum area in the city.

In 1911, following a detailed study of tuberculous diseases in Nottingham, the Medical Officer, Dr. Boobyer, singled out the most affected area, Narrow Marsh, as being:

The worst slum area of the city, if not in the Midland Counties. In one part there were 510 people to the acre, and most of the persons were in tenement houses. As to the explanation of that excessive incidence and mortality, it was due to poverty, physical and moral degradation, and many other things that followed in their train, especially overcrowding, intemperance and bestial filthiness.

The dishevelled and diseased inhabitants would cough, sneeze and spit on each other and thus add to the high rates of infection.

Dr. Boobyer was a long way from being the first to pass comment on the small web of slums clustering around Red Lion Street. Narrow Marsh, with its maze of dark alleyways, stinking side streets and common lodging houses was already infamous for its crime, poverty and general low life, the sewer of Nottingham, festering just a short walk from the city centre.

Alice, in a taped account of living conditions in Narrow Marsh, (ref: A81, available from Angel Row Local Studies Library) described the accommodation she remembers as a 7-year-old, just before World War 1:

One down and one up. No water, no gas, nowhere where you could wash or anything...When you went up to bed you took a candle with you...No heating and things like that...The toilet used to be across the yard, and the tap, the tap was in the yard.

Only one bedroom (for six). Course, mam'd have one wi' her, the baby. It was a great big bedroom, and there'd be one bed wi' mattress on. Mind you, we used to get in bed and (put) coats over us. We'd not many blankets, more big coats than owt...slept like logs.

The area nestled at the bottom of a cliff and was overlooked by the inmates of the County Gaol, many of whom may well have had family just yards away. Because of its large number of cheap lodging houses and its proximity to the city centre, Narrow Marsh became a Mecca for all manner of drop-out, who found refuge and 'lost' themselves there amongst their own kind. It attracted roaming tramps, thieves, vagabonds and criminals, including the notorious Charles Peace, once the most wanted men in the country.

After Jack the Ripper, Charlie Peace was the most infamous villain of the 19th century, eventually going to the gallows for the murder of a police officer. There persisted a rumour that Peace lost three fingers in Nottingham. He was said to have held up a butcher, who suddenly brought down his meat cleaver with the three digits and a gun duly following. The rumour isn't true: Peace lost the fingers during an accident in his youth.

Peace spent some time in Nottingham, lodging above a shoemaker's in Drury Hill. He was a most audacious criminal, openly removing a piano from The Tavern and carting it away for sale on a barrow. When the police arrived at his lodgings,

69. *Looking down on Narrow Marsh, the septic ulcer festering on the side of the city.*

he escaped through a fanlight in the roof and took up residence in Trinity Square. Following a major robbery in the Lace Market, the girls sharing Peace's accommodation could be seen parading in the streets wearing satin dresses well beyond their means.

With a warrant out for his arrest, Peace had a lucky escape. In a scene reminiscent of a spaghetti Western he was unexpectedly confronted by a brace of policemen in a barber's shop one day. The police made Peace's day by failing to recognise him under a swathe of lather, and the punk made good his escape, through a back entrance into Parliament Street. He then disappeared from Nottingham for good.

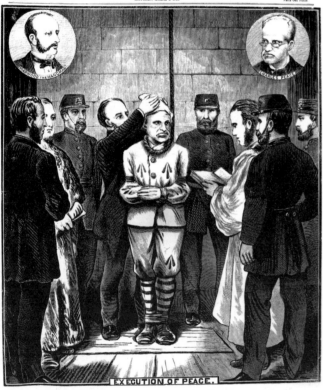

70. Charlie Peace, once the most wanted man in Britain for shooting a policeman was an audacious burglar who committed several crimes in Nottingham. Here Peace prepares to meet his maker.

The area supported no fewer than twelve pubs with probably the most famous, the Loggerheads, still serving pints today. They were open all day until 11.p.m. and drinking bouts often led to street brawls. Scraps might break out at any time but the police had to be most vigilant between 11.p.m. and midnight, after closing-time. A typical evening's entertainment, on March 24th 1907, was recorded in the *Evening Post* under the headline

Stabbing Sensation in Narrow Marsh.

Shortly after half past ten last night the people in Knotted-alley, Narrow-marsh, Nottingham, were disturbed by cries from the direction of No.23, where Samuel Chadwick, aged 61, a hawker, lives with his wife Emily, aged 51. Both were found to be bleeding profusely and to be suffering from severe wounds.

It is supposed the pair quarrelled and fought with knives, and the husband, who is unfortunately blind, appears to have come off the worse.

P.C.Horobin appeared on the scene, and man and wife were removed to the hospital. On examination the man was found to be suffering from wounds in the throat and abdomen of a rather serious nature, but he was quite conscious when admitted, and told the authorities that they were inflicted by his wife.

Mrs. Chadwick was found to have been stabbed in the face and arms, but she appeared to have escaped rather lightly in the struggle. She alleged that her husband had caused the injuries. They were both detained in the institution.

The inhabitants of Narrow Marsh feared nobody and took on all-comers, often clashing with gangs of youths from neighbouring districts, their courage bolstered following the consumption of seven or eight pints of strong ale:

Young bucks who lived on the outskirts of the city would come "down there" and were disappointed if they did not have a "bundle in" with someone before they returned home, or at least bore the honourable marks of the fracas.

Bare knuckle fights were frequently arranged and combatants set about each other on Thorneywood Mount or at the back of Clifton Pit. The brawlers often turned on the police if they tried to intervene and anybody knocked out or badly injured would be quickly and professionally fleeced by one of the many spectators.

Many of the poorly educated young men had no saving graces and were simply bullies and thugs. Two such louts, selected at random from a newspaper report at the end of the century, were Henry and James Davidson, described as labourers. They were just two of many and were charged with assaulting Elizabeth Pratt, a shopkeeper, who complained to a policeman about their behaviour. When he left they returned and gave Elizabeth a black eye. The newspaper report goes on to relate how the two brothers spent their spare time:

71. Before WW1 there over 500 people to the acre in Narrow Marsh.

The two defendants belonged to one of the roughest gangs in the city and at night would go to the top window of a house and shout out remarks to people in the street - Defendants were further charged with assaulting George Marshall, complainant alleging that they struck and kicked him until he was insensible, and that one of them threatened him with a knife.

They were each sent to prison for one month.

A considerable increase in the number of disturbances was noted during Goose Fair week (held in the Market Square until 1927). Hundreds of thieves and pickpockets would descend on Nottingham and take up residence in the cheap lodging houses to be found in Narrow Marsh. In 1899, Harriet Mason, of no fixed abode, was charged with stealing purses, the property of some persons unknown. She was spotted amongst the crowds on Beastmarket Hill moving in a 'suspicious manner'. When searched at the police station, several purses were found secreted about her body. Harriet defiantly told the magistrates that she 'did not give a f... and would do it again when she came out'. She was remanded in custody.

An incensed man, writing under the name 'outraged of Nottingham' complained to the local newspaper in 1897:

I passed through the fair on Saturday night, and there is no exaggeration in saying that I saw thousands of young people of both sexes - most of them under 21 - in various stages of intoxication;- from the frisky stage up to that of the beastly drunk... I never saw a more disgusting orgie of drunkenness and vice than Goose Fair presented at that particular occasion. It is likely to be the ruin of thousands of young people, and particularly of young girls....there is every year a large influx of low women and pickpockets from both Manchester and Birmingham.

These transients were themselves preyed on by

72. A solitary policeman is on hand to try and control the excited crowds at Goose Fair. One incensed observer of the fair wrote to the newspaper in 1897. 'I saw thousands of young people of both sexes - most of them under 21 - in various stages of intoxication from the frisky stage up to the beastly drunk... I never saw a more disgusting orgie of drunkenness and vice than Goose Fair presented...' Sounds like a good time was had by all!

73. *A scene from Goose Fair when still held in the Market Place. The crowded conditions could not have been more favourable for pickpockets who descended in droves upon the city from Manchester and Birmingham in search of easy pickings.*

the local men and women, who lured them into the narrow alleys and rabbit warrens just off Red Lion Street and Leen-Side. Here they would be set upon by members of a waiting gang and their own ill-gotten gains rifled.

In Narrow Marsh beat bobbies were habitually tormented and attacked, without provocation - a total of sixty-nine police were injured on duty in 1908, for example. The first objective, when attacking a member of the constabulary, was to relieve him of his whistle, in order to prevent him from summoning help. If this gambit was successful, the whistle was thrown well out of reach before the young thugs set about their 'sport'. One day a Sergeant Wild was attacked in such a manner, his whistle launched into space. The struggling policeman managed to follow its trajectory until it hit the ground beside Billy, a young man he knew well. Fending off the cowardly blows of the gang he shouted:

"Blow it, Billy, blow it!"

Billy sped towards Leen Side Police Station blowing the whistle for all he was worth. The 'cavalry' soon arrived to find the sergeant grimly holding on to two of his assailants. From that day on, Sergeant H. Wild, later to be promoted to the rank of Inspector, was known to everybody as "Billy Blowitt."

74. *The infamous Bush's Lodging House on Red Lion Street. Its guest book would have read like a criminal's 'Who's Who'.*

Police were often referred to by their individual nicknames, many not fit to print. The most famous was given to chief superintendent John Wise. The thinness of his neck was accentuated by the cut of the collar on uniforms before the Great War. He became known by everybody on the Marsh, locals and police alike, as "Duckneck".

75. In the nineteenth century washing lines would be lowered if a gang went on a job. When chased by the police gang members would duck under the lines.

When times were hard the washing was stolen from the lines by 'snowdroppers' and even the poles went missing, miraculously appearing on the market a few days later.

Members of the estimated nine adolescent gangs flourishing in the area, made use of clothes lines to hinder pursuing police. When a 'job' was imminent they lowered the clothes lines in the vicinity and ducked under them while making good their escape. Members of the constabulary were unable to give chase, as, in the dark, they risked running into the clothes lines pitched at about neck height.

If the police noticed beforehand that washing poles had been lowered they guessed that trouble was brewing and sometimes lowered them further to try and trip the fleet-footed urchins.

Nothing was safe. Clothes were stolen from lines by 'snowdroppers' and mats from doorways by 'tiger hunters'. Even the props holding up the clothes lines were removed and sold back to unsuspecting victims a few days later.

Crime was not, however, the sole province of young males. Edith Riley, a hosiery hand, stole and pawned no fewer than 59 shirts from her employer before being apprehended. The 26-year-old appeared in the dock with a baby in her arms. Both were imprisoned for one month.

Most charges against women were for theft, drunkenness or prostitution. 'Billy Blowitt', then just a constable, arrested Elizabeth Beaumont at the turn of the century. It was her 61st appearance on the charge of being drunk and disorderly. The habitual drunkard from Cox's Lane did not agree with the evidence and expressed some sort of grievance that no one could make head or tail of. With a fine deemed of little use in this case, Elizabeth took the familiar path to the cells to dry out for two weeks.

76. Elizabeth Raynor grew fat on the profits of prostitution from the girls in Narrow Marsh. Arrested three times in 1907 for keeping a brothel nearby at 15, Collin Street, she was fined a total of £20. On her fourth appearance Elizabeth was sentenced to one month's imprisonment with hard labour.

When in drink both men and women became violent. This report, about a basin cut, is from December 1895:

77. The Bottoms, Narrow Marsh. Boys would use carts to transport what remained of some of their neighbours home after drinking bouts and fights.

UNLAWFUL WOUNDING BY A WOMAN.

Julia Butler of Narrow Marsh was charged with 'unlawfully' wounding John Murray of Narrow-marsh on the 1st. Inst. Prosecutor stated that the prisoner last night struck him on the head with a basin which she broke with the force of the blow. Prisoner, he added, was subject to such fits and whilst they lasted she was incapable of taking care of herself. Prisoner was remanded for a week.

Beggars sought accommodation in Narrow Marsh on a Friday or Saturday, when the majority of workers were paid, and spent the weekend waylaying the locals in the town centre. On Sundays they set up their pitch outside the churches and chapels, invariably receiving a few pence from the spiritually uplifted. The rest of the week they begged from door to door.

Some were a bigger problem than others as they would both beg and steal. When in funds they hired a bed for the night in one of the many lodging houses. When out of funds, this being more often the case, they slept in outhouses. On one occasion, 29 tramps found ideal sleeping accommodation in a scrap merchant's yard; they dossed down in a giant disused boiler. They were discovered following complaints by the local residents, who could not sleep due to the snoring (reportedly in unison) being amplified by the boiler.

In winter the warm brick kilns provided excellent sleeping accommodation. Here tramps would strip off their filthy, lousy clothes and bury them in the hot, sulphurous kiln dust. This actually killed vermin and fumigated clothing. When no suitable doss could be found, tramps would sometimes deliberately break a window and wait to be accompanied to the prison cells.

Vagrant women caused a different kind of problem. Between 1900-14, two babies were born on the streets in Narrow Marsh, one after midnight in Red Lion Street, and the other by the roadside during a snowstorm, a policeman shielding the baby from the elements with his cape. A third baby was born at the local police station. We are happy to report that in all three cases 'mother and baby did well'.

Malnourished children supplemented their parent's income by earning pennies holding horses' heads while the owner had a drink or two. When this turned to nine or ten, boys rushed to Mr. Flint's, to borrow a handcart and drunks discovered lying on the pavement were pushed to the police station. Men badly beaten in one of the many fist fights would be transported home in like manner. The carters would be rewarded with a few pence.

Stealing was a way of life for many households and inevitably cases of juvenile offenders came before the courts. In 1900, Ann McLoughlin, (No. 78), 15, and under five feet tall, stole forty yards of serge from her employers and pledged six yards, double width, at Whitings' pawnshop. When she tried to pawn a further five yards at Poysers the counter staff became suspicious and informed the police.

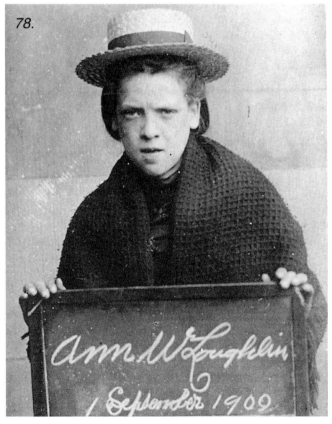

78.

A few years later, Alice, last seen sharing a bed with her sisters, was keeping lookout for her brother:

I remember one night, we was all in Bottom Street, and my brother says to me:
'I'm going in that chocolate factory tonight.'
'Oh', I says 'you be careful.'
and he says 'If a copper comes start singing "It's a long way to Tipperary"'. So he goes in him and his pal went in this here Cadbury's chocolate factory, and he went in and they were ever such a long while.
(A policeman on his beat passed by forcing tiny hearts to beat faster)
And he (the policeman)*stood back outside the factory and we all whistled "It's a long way to Tipperary", and our Harold says he'd seen his boots.*
'Oh,' I says 'Harold I nearly died'.
Anyway copper goes and I say "Come on, Harold, quick" and he gets out, oh, he'd got pockets of chocolate and oh, we didn't half have a party. I ate that much it made me sick.

79. *The Loggerheads is one of the few surviving pubs from the old Narrow Marsh.*

Alice remembers as a young girl sitting on the road by the pub and singing to the barrel-organ whose Italian players had just returned from town.

Some of the inhabitants did try to make an honest living. A number of Italians lodged in the area and would hire out barrel organs and wander the streets of Nottingham playing outside shops. On one occasion some tailors heated pennies in the workroom stove before throwing them to the unsuspecting entertainers.

When the day's work was over, the organ grinders returned to Red Lion Street, stopping outside the Loggerheads pub to play a free gig, a few songs for the children. The youngsters very quickly learnt the lyrics and danced and sang and screamed with excitement to the music of such songs as "*Who were you with last night?*" and "*Let's all go down the Strand.*"

Alice remembered the singing with affection:

We didn't play many games, only knocking at doors and running off. We always used to be sitting on the roads under Loggerheads and singing.

Other forms of entertainment included street musicians. A German band, three men with peaked caps playing brass instruments, were particularly popular. They played well - having plentiful supplies of wind from their diet of bread and onions - and followed the beggars around town.

Until the Protection of Animals Act passed in 1911, police had few powers to prevent the exploitation of animals. Before the legislation two men in Tyrolean costume wandered around the country with a performing bear and when in Nottingham they would took temporary lodgings in Narrow Marsh. They were rumoured to make a good living although It is unlikely the female bear thought so, as, if she did not accept the invitation to dance to the tunes played on the whistle and flute, she was mercilessly prodded with a pole until she found her rhythm again.

P.C. Wyvill was an animal lover, and, when he saw the mistreatment of the bear, in Shakespeare Street, he arrested her French owner, 42-year-old Pierre Huguet. The bear and her master were inseparable and both appeared together in Nottingham Guildhall. With the Frenchman's English being little better than the bear's, an interpreter was employed. As Pierre paid attention to the translated questions his partner laid down, indifferent to the proceedings. The main prosecution case was that the bear was being cruelly treated, having to perform somersaults whilst attached to a chain which passed through a ring piercing its cheek. Two of the magistrates examined the bear in the dock and noticed a hole in the skin and flesh of the cheek big enough to take two fingers. A vet testified that controlling the bear using the chain must have caused a great deal of pain.

The perplexed magistrates had no alternative other than to ask the couple to move on. The Frenchman was reluctant to do this but when asked by the interpreter if he would rather spend three months in prison, amongst general laughter he replied:

Ah, non.

At his next appearance, still refusing to leave, the Frenchman was fined 20 shillings. He replied that he had no money and refused to pay. The magistrates then faced a very tricky problem, how could they put the bear in prison? It was decided to take her to a menagerie at Colwick Hall until the fine was paid. Both bear and master left Nottingham a short time later.

Little now remains of the infamous 'Narrow Marsh', though visitors can still stroll along Red Lion Street (now Cliff Road), look up to the old County Gaol and pop into the Loggerheads for a pint, as so many villains once did.

80. Before the passing of the Protection of Animals Act in 1911 magistrates had few powers to prevent the obvious cruelty displayed here. The animal was expected to dance and turn somersaults whilst attached to a chain which passed through a ring pierced in the bear's cheek. The bear actually appeared in court along with her French master.

81. The final days of the old Narrow Marsh. Much was demolished in 1931.

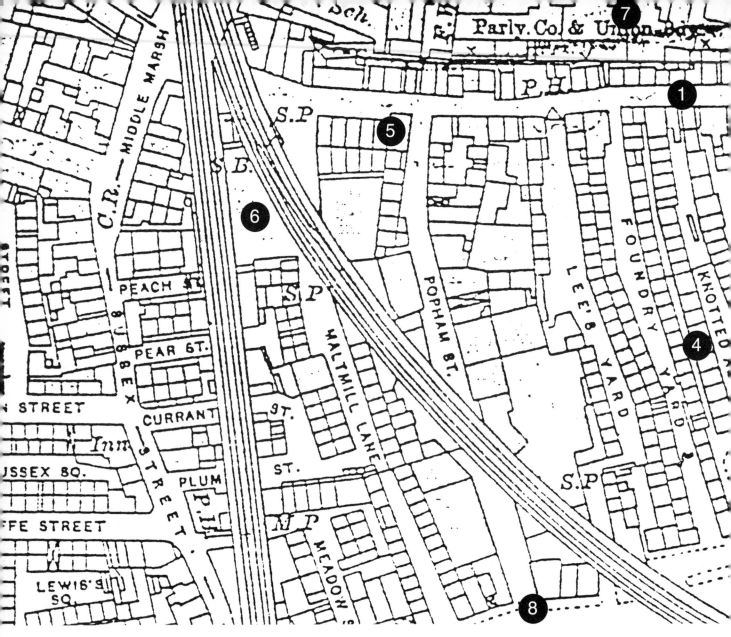

NARROW MARSH IN 1915

(1)　Red Lion Street, the former Narrow Marsh, now Cliff Road.

(2)　The Loggerheads, still serving pints today.

(3)　Many of the offenders repeatedly paraded before the courts gave their address as Knob Yard.

(4)　Knotted Alley where Samuel Chadwick 61, and his wife, 51, regularly fought each other. Emily tended to get the better of the battles as her husband was blind.

(5)　The infamous Bush's Lodging House whose guest book read like a criminals' 'Who's Who'.

(6)　The site of the Narrow Marsh murder that so horrified the people of Nottingham in 1905.

(7)　The Shire Hall and County Gaol. It was here that 'Nurse' Waddingham was sentenced to hang. Several of Nottingham's murderers, including Richard Parker are buried in the back yard.

(8)　Edward Glynn, insanely jealous of his former girlfriend stabbed her to death on Leen-Side/Canal Street. He showed no remorse and ate a hearty breakfast on the day of execution.

(9)　Leen-Side Police Station. Billy ran all the way blowing the police whistle for all he was worth.

RED LION STREET
Gt. Cntl. & Gt. N. Railway viaducts

(1)	Smith William, coal dealer
(11 &13)	Thorpe Wm. bho. Woodman
(15 & 22)	Bush Richard, reg. lodging houses
(21)	Elliott Henry, boot repairer
(23)	Collins Miss Mary Ann, shopkeeper
(29)	Wilkins Samuel
(31)	Lawson Christr. v. Old Red Lion
(33 & 35)	Murphy Thomas. jun. reg. lodging houses
(43)	Morley Issac
(49)	Burton George, shopkeeper
(51 & 53)	Cox Mrs. Sarah, reg. ldg. house
(55)	Gregory Mrs. Emma, shopkeeper
(57)	Conner Robert, reg. lodging house
(59)	Connor Mrs. Rose, v. Loggerheads
(61 & 63)	Conner Mrs. Rose, reg. lodging houses
(61)	Mundy George, chimney sweep
(63)	Voce John, coal dealer
(69 & 73)	Murphy George, reg. lodging houses
(71)	Murphy Mrs. Mary, reg. lodging houses
(71a)	Clements Geo. reg. lodging house
(73)	Murphy Geo. reg. lodging house
(75)	Coreoran Miss Mary, reg. lodging house
(77)	Riley Timothy, reg. lodging House
(79)	Moss Hy. registered lodging house
(81 & 83)	Pinder George Reuben, reg. lodging house
(87)	Conner Mrs. Rose, reg. lodging house

STAR & GARTER YARD

(89)	Lawson Michael, registered lodging house
(93 & 95)	Sisson Mrs, Mary, reg. lodging house
(97)	Sisson Mrs. Polly

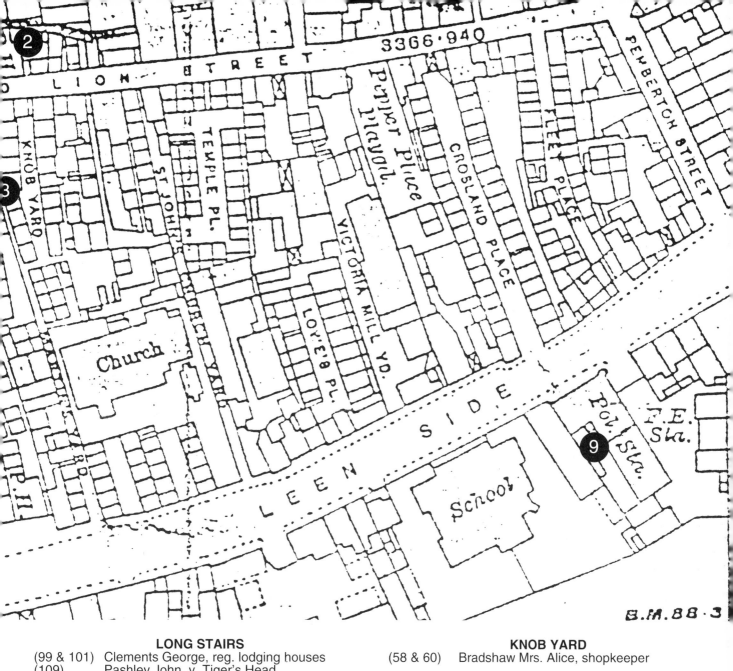

LONG STAIRS
(99 & 101) Clements George, reg. lodging houses
(109) Pashley John, v. Tiger's Head
(111 & 113) Collier Alexander, registered lodging house
(117 & 114) Gamble Samuel, coal dealer

PLUMPTRE SQUARE
(CROSS OVER)
LONDON ROAD
(114 & 117) Gamble Samuel, coal dealer

PEMBERTON STREET
(100) Robinson James Howard, v. King's Head

CROSLAND PLACE
(96) Field Mrs. Rachel, shopkeeper

RECREATION GROUND
(90) Murphy James, Travellers' Rest

NORTON PLACE
(86) Pinder Mrs. Annie, shopkeeper
(84) Goss William, fish frier
(80) Alford Edward, shopkeeper

TEMPLE PLACE
(74) Murphy Thomas, sen. reg. ldg. house keeper
(72) Corcoran Miss Mary, shopkeeper

ST. JOHN'S CHURCHYARD
BYRON YARD
(62 & 64) Murphy Thomas, jun. reg. lodging houses

KNOB YARD
(58 & 60) Bradshaw Mrs. Alice, shopkeeper

MARTIN'S YARD
(56) Wood John Wm. umbrella repairer
(54) Wachorn John, registered lodging house
(52) Brown Samuel, butcher
(50) Hammond Mrs. Florence, shopkeeper

TAYLOR'S YARD KNOTTED ALLEY
(44 & 46) Morley Issac, reg. lodging house

FOUNDRY YARD
(40) Church Army Mission (St. Johns)
(38) Howitt William, shopkeeper

LEOS YARD
Murphy & Morley, coal dealers
(36) Leonard Andrew, bho. White Lion

PEARSON'S YARD
(5) Brown Mrs. Elizh. registered lodging house
(32) Whetstone Mrs. Ellen, clothes dealer
(30) Whetstone Thomas, boot repairer
(26) Brown Geogre, registered lodging house

VAT YARD
(24) Borman Charles, dining rooms

POPHAM STREET
(22 & 15) Bush Richd, registered lodging house
(18) Bush Richard
(12) Welsh Thomas, shopkeeper

THE NARROW MARSH MURDERER

The motiveless killing of a young boy by the lodger

One of the most brutal crimes ever perpetrated within the city boundaries took place on 31st January 1905. The remains of Albert Matthews, just one month off his fifth birthday, were discovered by his mother in the family home, 1 Chapman's Yard, Malt Hill Lane, Narrow Marsh. He had been decapitated.

After the mother, the first person to witness the mutilation was a neighbour, Thomas Rourke, who had heard the shrill screams. Mrs. Matthews had not immediately realised what had happened and stood dazed, muttering to herself:

Oh, my boy, my boy; he's burnt to death or something.

Rourke then described the scene in his own words:

...it looked like a slaughter-house. And the poor kid - well I shouldn't see such a sight again for £20. He was gashed from throat to thigh, and his head was right under the sofa. I said: 'Oh, God, the kid's none been burnt; it's been murdered.' It was hacked about from head to foot.

There was never any doubt about the identity of the murderer. John Hutchinson, a 29-year-old labourer, had led a policeman to the house and admitted his guilt. He was described by Rourke as being as 'unconcerned as if nothing at all was amiss'. Greeting another neighbour with the question: 'How are you getting on Tommy?' he was informed that Tommy was all right. Hutchinson calmly said: 'I might as well have a smoke' and lit up. A pair of handcuffs were quickly fitted and the relaxed murderer was led docilely off to the police station.

The jury at the ensuing trial had a choice between three possible verdicts. Hutchinson claimed that the boy threw a poker at him and he acted in self-defence. If this was true there was the possibility of a manslaughter verdict, but owing to the mutilation of the body, this plea had very little chance of success. Defence counsel, Dr. Taraschand, pleaded for a verdict of guilty but insane. The prosecution were pressing for a charge of wilful murder. The sad undisputed details of the horrific crime are as follows:

After his discharge from the army in January 1905, Hutchinson returned to Nottingham to lodge with George Matthews and his family in Narrow Marsh.

On the day of the murder both Matthews and Hutchinson spent six hours, from 11.a.m. to 5.p.m. drinking at the Millers Arms, Agnes Street. Hutchinson returned to his lodgings, enabling Mrs. Matthews to go off to work, leaving her son, Albert, in the care of the drunken lodger.

At 7.p.m., Hutchinson returned to the Miller's Arms and told the child's father that he had put him to bed. Buying some cigarettes, Hutchinson told Matthews that he was going to visit his sister. He did not arrive. Instead he approached a policeman, admitted to a murder and led the constable to the scene of the crime. Unfortunately, Mrs. Matthews had returned home in the meantime and made the gruesome discovery. Hutchinson would not enter the house and appeared indifferent as to the severity of his crime.

The Trial

The Crown Court was packed as the prisoner was brought up. His appearance and attitude were vividly described in the *Evening Post* :

82. The first published photograph of the 'Narrow Marsh murderer' John Hutchinson. His plea of insanity was rejected but would almost certainly have been accepted today.

Unkempt, without collar or tie, with waistcoat thrown open - these things only went to intensify his naturally somewhat repulsive appearance, and his demeanour in the dock was wholly in keeping with the indifference and callousness that he has displayed all through.

When asked how he pleaded, Hutchinson's reply of '*not guilty*' was barely audible. He took a keen interest in the members of the jury who felt intimidated by his cold, blank, unblinking stare. This he occasionally directed at spectators in the packed galleries. His piercing eyes terrified all those who met his gaze as the accounts of his vicious attack and life history were laid bare before a hushed public. He seemed to show little interest or understanding of the proceedings which looked likely to end his life, and did not flinch when the murder weapon, a knife, was produced in evidence. He only appeared to focus his attention, sitting bolt upright, his arms tightly folded, when listening to the testimonies of the boy's parents, Mr. and Mrs. Matthews.

George Matthews, replying to a question from the defence, agreed that Hutchinson seemed to get on well with his son. Other police witnesses testified as to how calm Hutchinson had remained since the murder. A Dr. Taylor argued that the defendant was sober and rational and knew that what he had done was wrong. He found no evidence of insanity.

For the defence, Dr. Taraschand contested that the crime was committed by Hutchinson, an 'epileptic maniac', whilst he was having a fit. This was refuted by Dr. Taylor, who argued that anybody in such a state would not recall what he had done; Hutchinson had led a policeman to the house and told him details of the crime.

Much play was made of the apparent indifference and lack of remorse shown by the murderer. The defence was permitted to introduce records of the prisoner's family to try and prove that he was inherently insane.

Four of his relatives, on his mother's side, had committed suicide. Living in Carlton had driven them to despair. Thomas Norman hanged himself there in 1884. William Hutchinson followed his example in the same place in 1892. Anne Perry, once again in Carlton, drowned herself and Annie Smith took her own life in similar fashion in Burton Joyce. Two other members of the family were inmates of the Notts County Lunatic Asylum.

Arthur Hutchinson, the prisoner's father, testified that at the age of 6, his son had been butted on the back of the head by a sheep. At the age of 21, his head was trampled on by a horse. In the summer of 1897 he had suffered several fits.

A number of other witnesses, from both the army and civvy street, testified as to the defendant's bizarre behaviour; he had tried to strangle his brother and seemed convinced that rats lived on the mess wall. All the witnesses confirmed that Hutchinson suffered regularly from fits and seizures.

Mr. Edge, a physician and surgeon from Basford, was convinced that the defendant was insane. He described Hutchinson as a man with very slow thinking power. When asked if, after striking the child and finding him dead, an epileptic fit may have been invoked, the physician replied '*Yes*'. When questioned further as to whether this may have led to the mutilation of the body, he replied; '*Yes, I think it might.*'

To counter these arguments, Dr. O'Kell, the medical officer at Bagthorpe Prison, said that he had observed Hutchinson every day since his arrest and was convinced that he was perfectly sane.

In his summing up the defence counsel argued that Hutchinson was insane and therefore not responsible for his actions for the following reasons: there was a history of insanity in the family; the accused was prone to fits; there was no motive for the crime; the mutilation was so horrendous that no sane man would have carried it out; he had shown no remorse whatsoever.

The judge's summing up appeared to favour the case for the prosecution and the jury returned their verdict after just twenty minutes. John Hutchinson was found guilty of wilful murder.

The bedraggled prisoner seemed unmoved, and when asked if he had anything to say why sentence of death should not be passed on him, he sullenly repeated three times the word '*no*'.

Donning his black cap, his Lordship, Mr. Justice Phillimore addressed the prisoner:

The jury have found you guilty of this crime; that is to say, that there was no doubt that you had done this poor child to death. The only question was whether or not you were responsible for your act. All that can be said or done upon your behalf has been done; the jury have considered it, and have found that you were responsible. It is their responsibility to say so, and I should like to associate myself with them. I think they are quite right. I am glad to think that you have understanding, and I hope that you will employ the time in a rational way, in a humble way, and in a contrite and sorrowful way, that you will listen to the ministrations of the chaplain of the gaol and that you prepare to meet your maker.

It is unlikely that Hutchinson understood much of the message from the judge. He did understand that he was sentenced to death and his last words in court were more blunt and direct than those of Mr. Justice Phillimore. Staring icily with contempt, he shouted at the jury:

F... the lot of you.

The child killer fell under the spell of the visiting chaplain and was very influenced by his teachings. The Bishop of Southwell made a special trip to confirm him in his cell. Outwardly calm, he walked to the scaffold with a firm step. John Hutchinson was hanged at Bagthorpe gaol on 29th March 1905, three weeks after his trial. The small crowd did not even see the black flag hoisted as this custom had recently been abolished.

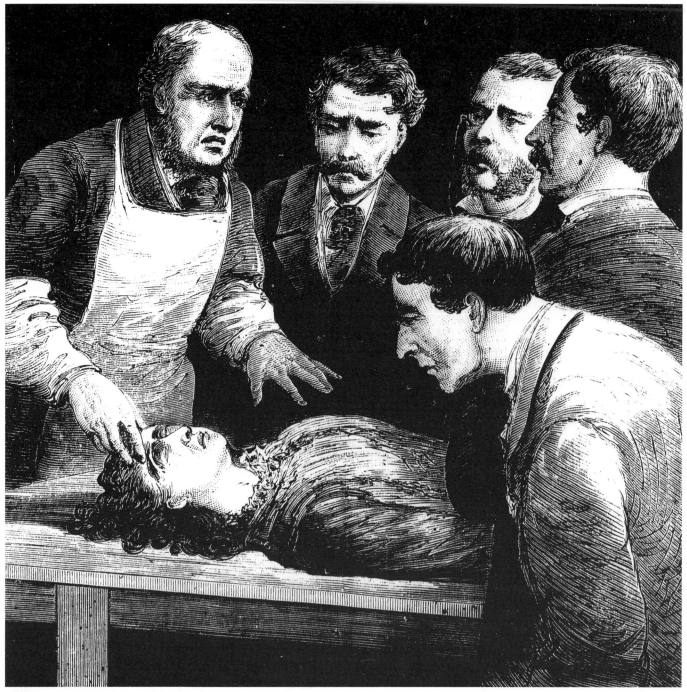

83. Post mortems would sometimes take place in the local pub. All too frequently pathologists were examining the corpses of young children and adults, the victims of crime, although this was often difficult to prove.

THE FINAL EXIT

Hutchinson's family was not unique in its suicidal habits. Conditions were so difficult, particularly for the Victorian poor, that many saw only one way out.

Suicide was an offence against the crown until the influence of psychoanalysis altered popular opinion on the subject.

At the turn of the century the most common methods of suicide in Nottingham included the following: cutting the throat with a razor or scissors; stabbing; drowning in a canal or in the River Trent; shooting; jumping off a railway bridge; taking carbolic acid; jumping from a window.

One man, to make doubly certain, slit his throat and jumped through an attic window.

Other causes of death, not so common today, included: accidentally slipping while riding on the footboard of a train; injuries caused by being kicked by a horse, tossed by a bull; being pushed under the wheel of a passing van by man unknown; injuries to head caused by a falling tree; drowning in the canal (pushed in by another boy); slipping on stairs; chronic alcoholism; burns caused by clothes catching fire; overdose of Chocal taken in excessive quantity by way of habit.

A fairly high percentage of deaths recorded at Leen-Side mortuary were blatant suicides.

DEATHS RECORDED AT THE CORONER'S COURT, LEEN-SIDE JANUARY- MARCH 1905.

NAME	AGE	CAUSE OF DEATH
Charlotte Dale	62	Burns caused by falling downstairs while alone.
Albert Knowles	4mths	Suffocation due to regurgitated vomit.
Ellen Eyre	7wks	Pneumonia in left lung.
Thomas Seymours	27	Rupture of spleen by being accidentally caught between a travelling crane and a girder.
Sarah Whitehead	58	Heart failure and alcoholic cirrhosis of the liver.
James Wakefield	57	Suicide by drowning himself in water butt (U.M.).
Margaret Nicholson	53	Cerebral haemorrhage.
Elizabeth Lambert	83	Heart failure.
Albert Matthews	5	Wilful murder [by John Hutchinson].
Jane Moore	48	Suicide by carbolic acid.
Annie Haywood	4mths	Suffocation due to regurgitated vomit.
Harry Warsop	13mths	Acute pneumonia.
Timothy Gregory	40	Septicaemia due to accidental fracture of left leg.
Lewis Morris	13mths	Pneumonia and pleurisy.
Charles Turland	3wks	Asphyxia due to being too closely covered in bed.
George Wright	4mths	Suffocation by being left in his crib on his belly.
May Baseley	31	Suicide by drowning (U.M.).
Esau Perry	46	Injuries caused by fall in Clifton pit.
Wilford Groves	4	Pneumonia following measles and want of medical attention.
Samuel Harston	77	Bronchitis.
Edward Messon	11days	Suffocation while in bed with parents.
Albert Ashley	6wks	Suffocation due to regurgitated vomit.
Ada Collins	32	Suicide by drowning.
Harriet Davis	2y 6m	Run over by a bus.
Elizabeth Blackwell	52	Cerebral haemorrhage.
Elizabeth Briggs	3y10m	Whooping cough.
Eliza Large	41	Shock due to burns caused by a paraffin stove.
Frank Dunford	25	Suicide by hanging.
James Calow	37	Suicide by hanging.
George Carlisle	41	Suicide by drowning.
Christopher Astill	3	Meningitis.
Ernest Wilkinson	6	Acute peritonitis.
Ethel Grainger	4mths	Suffocation while in bed with parents.
Charley Swift	56	Heart failure due to chronic alcoholism.
John Hutchinson	29	Dislocation of the neck by hanging [for the murder of Albert Matthews].

(U.M. = unsound mind)

Many of the above were not resident in Narrow Marsh, but lived in the neighbourhood. If the infant mortality figures are included, life expectancy for Central Nottingham was 27.

84. Life was so harsh that many took an early exit. At the turn of the century the most common forms of suicide included: cutting the throat with a razor or scissors; drowning in a canal or the Trent; jumping from a railway bridge or a window and taking carbolic acid.

TROUBLESOME TRAMPS

85. Joseph Pegg. Tramps were often charged with having no visible means of support. Joseph was discharged. He did not represent a great threat to the community with only two previous convictions:- stealing a bottle of lemon curd and some biscuits.

The police had no problem finding charges for those whose faces did not fit. You could be arrested for being an idle and disorderly person; an incorrigible rogue; a beggar wandering abroad; water lily thief or purloiner of growing cabbages.

In 1878 Joseph Baker, James Palmer and William Hall, three tramps, were charged with sleeping on two straw stacks on the Alfreton Road. Baker and Palmer were imprisoned for three days, and Hall, who had just completed a seven year stretch, was sent down for one month. However harsh were prison conditions, many tramps preferred them to workhouses and would deliberately commit minor offences in order to be gaoled. At a council meeting in 1914, workhouse guardians were accused of treating tramps like vermin and of making them feel loathed by everyone. At the same meeting, the treatment of tramps was condemned as 'a barbarous relic of the Oliver Twist period'.

In defence of the guardians, Mr. Hopkinson argued that Nottingham treated tramps better than many other places and cited, as an example of this better treatment, the provision of gruel instead of bread and water. Tramps resented being made to work, he said, and would not do so unless strictly supervised. In support of this, Mr. T. Ward told the meeting that he had seen tramps, supposed to be working on the land, apparently *holding a convivial*, a remark which drew much laughter. Mr. Ward further observed that certain tramps would arrive at the workhouse with utmost regularity and would often come to the door and ask: *Is my bed ready aired?* (more laughter). The speaker went on to liken them to commercial travellers arriving at a hotel.

Tramps were real knights of the road, walking from town to town and city to city. One member of their fraternity scratched the following lines on the wall at Bagthorpe workhouse:

The sailor loves his ship,
The soldier loves his camp,
But give me the country lanes
And I will die a tramp.

A typical example of their independent attitude was recorded in *The Evening News* under the headline **'Troublesome Tramp'**:

Bernard Baglion, labourer, was charged with refusing to work at the Bagthorpe Workhouse on the 7th inst. with wilfully damaging two cell doors, to the extent of 15s. and with assaulting Mr. H Finch, the tramp master. He admitted the damage, but denied the other charges. Mr. Finch said that he was given a task which he refused to perform. He was put in a cell, but broke the door and got out, attacking witness with a hammer...he smashed an outer door and bolted into the field adjoining the workhouse, where he was captured. Baglion said he never struck Mr. Finch at all, but that the latter struck him. He added that the tramp master had no right to detain him when he wanted to go. He was sent to prison for the damage and a similar term on the charge of refusing to work.

86. Joseph Graham a pauper who listed his address as the workhouse. Took to crime late in life when stealing bed linen.

87. The workhouse, the last resort for desperate paupers. They continued well into the twentieth century and many preferred a short spell in prison to the austere conditions of the most depressing of institutions.

88. York street workhouse in 1896. It was demolished a short time later to make way for Victoria Station.

MORE MURDER

89. Nearly all the victims of murder cases in Nottingham were women. They were killed by men known to them, often with a cut-throat razor.

THE HYSON GREEN MURDERER

With the certainty of death just a few days away, some condemned men turn to religion, others confess their crimes and a few continue to protest their innocence. Walter Smith, the Hyson Green murderer, insisted to the very end that he would go to the gallows a wronged man.

In December 1893 a beautiful 25-year-old nurse called round to visit Smith, who was renting rooms in Abbot's factory on Forest Street, Hyson Green. The 32-year-old self-employed fitter was a casual acquaintance Catherine Cross had met during the Christmas break from her hospital in Liverpool. Catherine was engaged to be married.

Quite what happened in the factory we shall never know. Three shots were fired and the wounded Catherine staggered from one of the rooms. She managed to cling on to life for two more days before succumbing to injuries caused by a bullet, which entered her body via the chin and lodged in the spine. Before she died, Catherine indicated that the shooting was an accident and Smith concurred, maintaining this story right until the white cap was adjusted over his head. The problem with Smith's defence centred on the fact that a total of three shots had been discharged. One, conceivably, may have been an accident, but three was more than carelessness.

The prosecution found it difficult to prove a motive, perhaps Catherine had refused Smith's advances. She had earlier made it clear that their relationship was purely platonic, when refusing his invitation to ride tandem.

The jury took just over an hour to find Smith guilty. When beseeched by his mother to give himself up to God, he replied:

I would rather stop here for I am innocent of any intention even to harm her. To think I should be buried tomorrow like a dog.

Thousands gathered outside the new prison on 27th March 1894 for the first of the fifteen hangings which took place at Bagthorpe Prison. Barely sixty seconds passed between Smith emerging from the main block and his neck being broken. Death was almost instantaneous and the crowd slowly made their way home after the black flag was raised at around 8.a.m.

A DOUBLE EXECUTION

Two years later the last double hanging in Nottingham was held at Bagthorpe Prison. The penultimate such execution, in 1831, was that of William Reynolds and William Marshall, who 'danced the Paddington frisk' before an estimated crowd of some 20,000. The two Williams were hanged for the rape of 22-year-old Mary Ann Lord who was seized by four young men and raped in Wood Street. She was warned that if she told anybody about the assault she would be thrown down a well. The young bullies hadn't reckoned on her courage. One of the perpetrators was sentenced to transportation for life but after many appeals Reynolds and Marshall were hanged. Both appeared indifferent as to their fate.

Some sixty five years later, two men who had never met were dispatched into the unknown at exactly the same time, 8.a.m. on August 11th 1896. In contrast to the high profile rape case above, the deaths of Samuel Wilkinson and John Rose were witnessed by a mere handful of officials. Their bodies were left to hang for one hour. Both crimes were paradigms of their type, one a murder for greed and the other for domestic reasons.

Samuel Wilkinson, 48, listed his profession as that of gardener, although professional thief might have been more appropriate. During a burglary in Arnold he murdered a woman of 73 by beating her about the head with a poker as she tried to prevent him stealing a silver watch and several sovereigns. He was spotted the next day in the Royal Oak, in Broad Marsh, but quickly fled to Manchester where he disposed of the stolen goods around local pubs. Following an abortive attempt at stealing bottles of spirits, he was captured and imprisoned in Strangeways. Communication between the various police forces was then improving and a diligent police officer recognised their prisoner as the man wanted in Nottingham. He was dispatched to Nottingham forthwith and to the hereafter a little later.

John Rose's murder of his wife Mary was a typical 'domestic'. Mary moaned at John because he was unemployed; John drank because he was unemployed, and drank more because at 53, he could not find work in his profession as a baker. Mary resented giving the little money she earned as a lace-maker to John because he only drank it.

Mary moaned, John drank.

John slashed her throat and then turned the razor on himself. He was found alive but the jury did not believe his defence that his wife had slashed him and then herself.

The black flag was raised one minute after the morning drop.

A CASE OF POSSESSIVE JEALOUSY

The next Nottingham man to hang in the same year, Joseph Allcock, was guilty of the same crime: he murdered his wife Emma, the mother of their two sons, Joseph, 7 and George, 5.

The couple had spent eight unhappy years together. Joseph was possessively jealous of his wife and imagined she was having affairs with every Tom, Colin or Roger in Bulwell. On 17th September Joseph's wife refused to share a bedroom with him. If she wouldn't sleep with him he was determined she would sleep with nobody else. After stabbing her with a pick blade, he cut her throat and then gave himself up at Basford Police Station. The whole episode had been heard by a neighbour through the thin walls of her terraced house in Key Street. At least the collier had spared the lives of his two sons. He was baptised on 21st December 1896 and hanged two days later. He walked to the scaffold, deathly pale but unflinching.

90. *Rear view of the Shire Hall which can be visited throughout the year (photograph courtesy of the Galleries of Justice).*

THE CONDEMNED MAN ATE A HEARTY BREAKFAST

Ten years later, Edward Glynn ate a hearty breakfast. Minutes from execution he seemed indifferent to his fate. He had been convicted for the murder in Leen-Side, Narrow Marsh, of Jane Gamble, an ex-girlfriend. He so viciously stabbed her the blade of the knife broke off and a piece of metal 2" long and half an inch wide was embedded near the vertebrae. Jane managed to live until the early hours of the following morning but succumbed to her horrendous injuries. Another case of a violently jealous man lashing out in drink. Whilst awaiting his execution Glynn admitted his guilt. He was hanged on 7th August 1906.

FOUR LIVES CUT SHORT IN ARNOLD

As he left his home in Robinson's yard, Arnold, Mr. Marriot's attention was drawn by a knocking on his neighbour's window. It was a loud and frantic knocking, a one-handed knock, coming from a man whose occupied hand was clutching a blood-stained red cloth to his throat. Knowing his neighbour's instability, which led to violent, tempestuous domestic rows which were the talk of the street, Marriot feared the worst. Rushing into the house he quickly bypassed Atherley, the man whose throat had been cut, and raced upstairs to search for his common-law wife and three young children. He found them in the bedroom.

All four were stretched out on the bed, their throats deeply gashed with clothes covering their bloodied contorted faces. Two blood-stained razors and one hammer lay on the floor.

Atherley confessed to the arresting officer:

I killed them at 3 o'clock this morning. I broke the razor over them. I fetched another razor to do myself which I afterwards threw at the back of the bed. I lay lingering until I rapped the window for Marriott.

As Atherley was found to be unrepresented at his subsequent trial, the case had to be adjourned for a few hours. With only this short time to work out a defence the hastily appointed counsel argued that his client was insane at the time of the murders. This plea being backed by the premise that Atherley had served abroad in the services and, in 1909, it was believed that men who had been stationed in hot countries were more likely to suffer from epilepsy. The ex-soldier had obviously committed the crime during a fit!

Atherley seemed to contradict this defence when he blamed his crime on jealousy - another insecure man who believed his wife was 'playing away'. Showing no remorse, he was hanged by Pierrepoint on 14th December 1909.

91. Drink was involved in many of the cases and often the murderer gave himself up or attempted suicide.

ANGEL OR DEVIL IN DISGUISE?

92. A rather flattering photo of 'Nurse' Waddingham as she would greet the new arrivals in her private nursing home in Sherwood. Waddingham had no medical qualifications but, through experience, was familiar with handling drugs such as morphine.

Hucknall's main claim to fame is the presence in the church of the remains of Lord Byron. In the annals of Nottingham crime, the small former mining town, some seven miles to the north of the city, is best remembered as the birthplace of Dorothea Waddingham, later to become infamous as 'Nurse' Waddingham.

Dorothy, as she liked to be known, was born of poor parents at the turn of the century. Her early life was unremarkable, she kept a low profile, both at school and in the inevitable factory job that followed. She was not, however, a contented soul and wanted more than the drudgery and despair that were the lot of working-class women in the early years of this century. Accordingly Dorothy, in her early twenties, seized the opportunity to change her life, swapping her dead-end job as a piece of factory fodder for a post as a ward-maid in the workhouse infirmary at Burton-upon-Trent. It was here that she gained some knowledge of the caring profession, though she never qualified and was not therefore entitled to the nomenclature 'nurse'.

It was in the town renowned for its breweries that Dorothy met her first husband, Thomas Leech. Were the couple ever seen walking out together most passers-by would have considered them to be a nurse in the company of her patient. Thomas Leech was almost twice as old as Dorothy and in very poor health, though his reproductive faculties stood up to medical examination. Over the next eight years Dorothy gave birth to three children. They initially lived with Thomas' sister but money was so short that Dorothy resorted to crime to try and make life a little easier for her young children and sick, penniless husband.

The first time the young mother came to the attention of the police was in 1925, when she was charged with obtaining two dresses by deception. Undaunted, Dorothy persevered in her life of crime, raising the stakes far above those of the petty criminal by attempting to obtain goods to the value of £500 with a bounced cheque. The two years' probation she consequently received did not however deter her. With rent outstanding by nearly two years and a bare cupboard, Dorothy stole and pawned a gold wristlet watch from her children's maid, to whom she already owed £9 in unpaid wages! For this effort she was rewarded with 10s 6d and three months' hard labour. It was then things became really tough: her husband, Thomas Leech, died of throat cancer. The 'nurse' was left with a criminal record and three young children.

Now living at 57 North Road, West Bridgford and having re-adopted her maiden name, Dorothy was soon back in the swing of things. Not short of admirers, she quickly teamed up with a man closer to her own age. Ronald Sullivan, the holder of the Military Medal for gallantry for rescuing an officer under fire in WW1, found domestic flak somewhat harder to handle and had split from his wife. He was not disenchanted with family life, however, and only too pleased to join forces with Dorothy and her children.

The couple took up residence in Devon Drive, Sherwood, with the intention of running a nursing home for 'aged, invalid, helpless old people'. An intermediary, looking for accommodation for two people who matched this description, had the misfortune to come across the address and to knock on their door one afternoon in January 1935.

93. Ada and Loisa Baguley, daughter and mother, both poisoned for their inheritance shortly after arriving in Nottingham. Waddingham was found guilty of the murder of the daughter and the crown did not proceed with the case of Loisa Baguley.

Loisa and Ada Baguley, mother and daughter, were in desperate need of loving care and attention. At 87, Loisa, was more mobile than her 50-year-old daughter, who suffered from creeping paralysis and, at sixteen stone, was grossly overweight. The mother, a widow for six years, was anxious to find someone to help her care for her daughter. She was not so desperate, however, as to part easily with the little precious cash at her disposal and drove a hard bargain. Dorothy, now with an extra mouth to feed following the birth of a new son, was eager for any source of income, and agreed to put the Baguleys up at the ridiculously low fee of 30s each per week. For this paltry amount of money they were entitled to board, lodging, nursing and attendance, as well as a weekly ration of brandy. Having struck such a good deal, the two women wasted little time in moving to Sherwood from Burton Joyce.

After just a few weeks 'Nurse' Waddingham began to realise the awful financial mess she had been responsible for putting her family in. She would often complain about how little the infirm couple were paying and determined to renegotiate the deal. If they were to avoid the workhouse, the Baguley's would have to pay extra. Because they were reasonably happy in their new home, the invalids, after much wheeling and dealing, reached a compromise with Ronald Sullivan and the self-styled nurse.

Ada's total assets were about £1,600, the bulk of which was left by her father. Ada had intended to leave residual monies, at her death, to Fred Gilbert, her cousin, who had also been her sweetheart in happier times. Now, pragmatically, she made alternative arrangements. A new will, drafted with the help of the Baguley's solicitors, was signed in the presence of Ronald Sullivan. An edited version reads as follows:

This is the last will and testament of me, Ada Louise Baguley, of no.32, Devon Drive in the city of Nottingham...I give, devise and bequeath all my estate and effects whatsoever and wheresoever both real and personal unto and equally between Dorothea Nancy Waddingham and Ronald Joseph Sullivan ... for their use absolutely in consideration of the fact that they have undertaken to look after me and my mother, Loisa Baguley, for and during our joint lives.

I revoke all former wills, etc.

In witness whereof I have hereunto set my hand this 7th day of May 1935.

Five days later her mother Loisa was found dead.

Despite the short period between the re-negotiations, the new will and the death, nobody suspected foul play. Loisa Baguley's funeral was attended by Sullivan and an appropriately attentive Waddingham. Ada's wheelchair was pushed by former boyfriend and prior beneficiary, Fred Gilbert. Loisa was laid to rest - for the time being - in Caunton churchyard.

Sullivan and Waddingham did not actually benefit from the death, indeed they lost money, their weekly income being reduced from £3 to 30s. The only way they could be sure of gaining was if Ada followed her mother to an early grave. Ada duly obliged just four months later.

94. Ada Baguley whose life was blighted by ill-health and finally terminated by the nurse from hell. Ada decided to call off her engagement because of creeping paralysis. When she arrived as a 50-year-old at the nursing home she weighed almost 16-stone and spent most of her time in a wheelchair.

'Nurse' Waddingham's later statement about the death runs as follows:

I have never given Miss Baguley any morphia. I have never had any in the house. I had to keep her outside as she smelt horribly. She had a good dinner of pork on Tuesday, 10th Sept., and she asked for more and she had a second helping. She asked me to bring her in about 7.p.m. and I gave her two arrowroot biscuits and a cup of milk. She used to eat aspirins like toffee. I gave her medicine about 8.p.m. prescribed by Dr. Mansfield. It was the last dose. The medicine often made her choke. She was to take this medicine three times a day but I only gave her it at night. She has had medicine all the time she has been with me, prescribed by Dr. Jacobs and Dr. Mansfield. I put her to bed just gone 8.p.m. Joe Sullivan helped to lift her in. She spoke to having a headache and cried, and seemed very depressed. About 2.20.a.m. I went down to see her and noticed her eyes were open. I said to her:

'Are you awake, Ada? Your eyes are open: are you all right?'

Her eyes seemed bright. I took her pulse and it was not 30. She shut her eyes and to my knowledge did not open them again. I called Mr. Sullivan down and said to him:

'Look at Ada, what do you think of her? I don't know what to make of her.'

On and off we both remained with her and as she got no worse I decided not to send for Dr. Mansfield till surgery hours. She was breathing fast and seemed to rattle about 8.30.a.m. and there was all mucus down her face and in her nose. Mr. Sullivan rang for the doctor at my request about 8.50. a.m., but he was out. Miss Baguley died just after 10.a.m. Mr. Sullivan kept watching her while we were waiting for the doctor and just about 10.a.m. he said me:

'She has about gone.'

I went to her and found that she was dead...

When Dr. Mansfield arrived about midday he certified Ada as having died from *cerebral haemorrhage due to cardiovascular degeneration*.

Despite the fact that friends had seen her in reasonable health a few days previously, there appeared nothing immediately suspicious about this second death in four months. In the 1930s nurses were considered beyond reproach and nobody pointed a finger of suspicion at Waddingham. She made the mistake of doing that herself.

August 29th., 1935.

To Dr. Mansfield,
I desire to be cremated at my death for health's sake and it is my wish to remain with Nurse and my last wish is that my relatives shall not know of my death.

(Signed)

A.L.BAGULEY

R.J.SULLIVAN.

An extraordinary letter, (above) drafted by Sullivan, and purporting to have been signed by Ada some two weeks previously, could not have failed to set alarm bells ringing.

With just one in a hundred electing to be cremated at that time it did not need an over-suspicious mind to gauge that all was far from innocent .

The crematorium referee, Dr. Banks, who must have heard about the letter, became suspicious and Ada's body was removed to the mortuary. During the post-mortem Dr. Taylor found morphine in the stomach and other internal organs.

At the end of September, the body of Ada's mother was exhumed and once again traces of morphine found. Were the deaths accidental or by design? Who administered the drug? Throughout January and February 1936, first the Coroner's Court and later the Crown Court sought to resolve these questions. The public, through extensive press coverage, showed a tremendous appetite for the case and there was not one vacant seat throughout the trial.

In the Coroner's Court 'Nurse' Waddingham interrupted the proceedings on several occasions, sometimes by muttering to herself phrases such as *It is not fair* and *It is a lie*, at others she was openly defiant. Clearly incensed at the amount of attention given to the will she would often jump up to put her case:

95. The courtroom at the Shire Hall, now open to the public at the Galleries of Justice.

MRS. WADDINGHAM: (shouting) *Why bring the will up every time? You have investigated more into the will than into the death! It is not fair.*

It is not fair to go on about the will as you are! It is not fair to set the jury against me! You won't let my solicitor do anything! You speak as if I have done wrong - I have not.

CORONER: (soothingly) *I fully appreciate it is distressing.*

MRS. WADDINGHAM: *It is more than distressing! It is wicked! You never say a word in my favour - not one. You can have the money and use it to clear my name.*

Dorothy then stormed out of the court. The first inquest (on the death of Ada) terminated on January 30th. Dorothy was not in the court but in the corridor when the jury's verdict was announced:

The unanimous verdict of the jury is that Ada Baguley met her death by a fatal dose of morphine or heroin, or both, and their considered opinion is that there was a joint conspiracy. Our verdict is one of wilful murder against Ronald Sullivan and Nurse Waddingham.

Dorothy's screams filled the courthouse. She had to be forcibly restrained.

Both Ronald Sullivan and Nurse Waddingham were arrested. Waddingham was held at Winson Green (Birmingham) and Sullivan at Lincoln. They were jointly charged with the murders of Miss Ada Louisa Baguley, on September 11th 1935 and of Mrs. Loisa Baguley (mother of Miss) on May 12th 1935. The address of each of the accused was given as 32, Devon Drive, and their ages as 41 and 34, respectively.

96. Ronald Sullivan and Dorothea Waddingham in happier times. The judge ordered Sullivan to be found not guilty as there was no evidence against him.

84

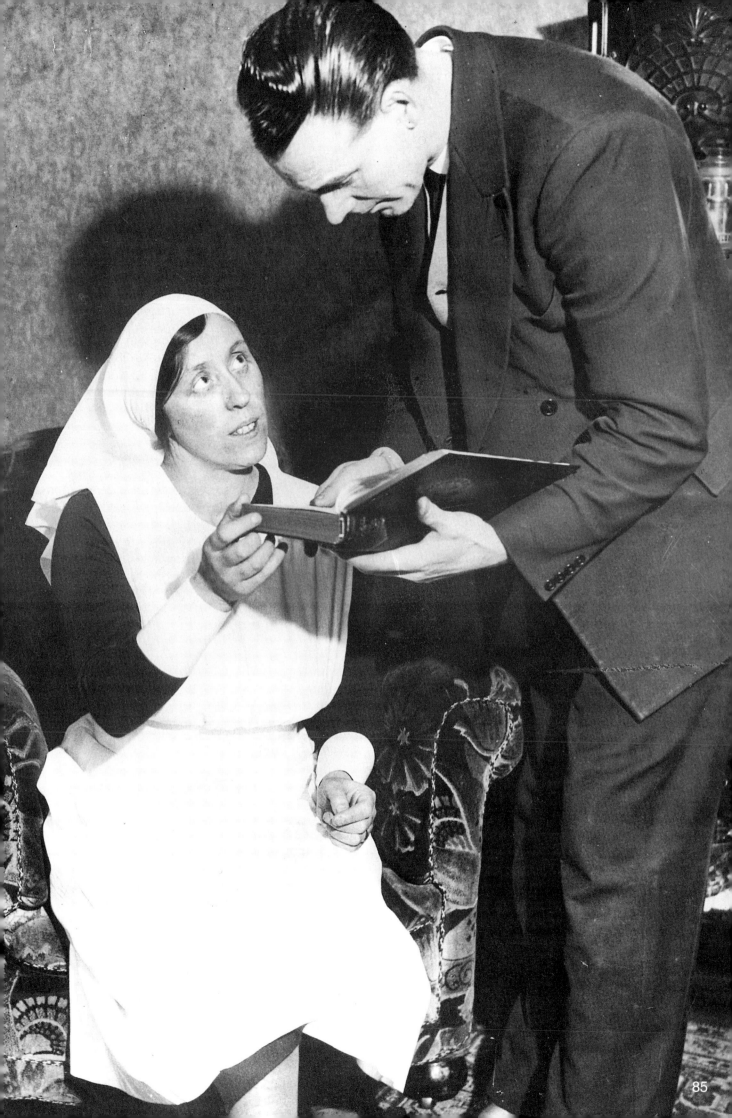

The case opened in February with queues forming outside the Guildhall hours before the 12 o'clock commencement of proceedings and all spare places in the courtroom were speedily filled.

Following the trauma in the Coroner's Court, Waddingham seemed to have recovered her composure and appeared more relaxed. She wore a smart black coat embellished with maroon accessories of hat and scarf. Sullivan sported a blue suit, white shirt and black tie. The trial was complicated by the fact that Dorothy brought her recently born fifth child into court on the first day of proceedings, possibly to elicit sympathy. For the rest of the trial the baby was cared for at Winson Green prison.

The whole case centred around the morphia: where it had originated and who administered the deadly doses. Although Waddingham denied giving the drug to either of the Baguleys, she admitted to having previously administered morphia to a Mrs. Kemp, a former 'patient'. According to Sullivan, the unfinished bottle was left in the bathroom.

Following a succession of expert medical testimonies the judge began to wonder out loud if Sullivan had a case to answer:

THE JUDGE: *What evidence do you say there is against the man?*

MR. BIRKETT: (prosecution): *There is no direct evidence against the prisoner Sullivan of possession. There is no direct evidence against him of administration of morphia. There is evidence for the jury to consider against the female prisoner both of possession and administration.*

THE JUDGE: *Yes, I am not dealing with her.*

Following unsuccessful arguments by the prosecution that the couple had 'a common aim' the jury was ordered to find Sullivan 'not guilty' and he was taken down, although not allowed to leave. This left Dorothea Waddingham alone in the dock and now it was her turn to give evidence. Friendless and vulnerable she gave her answers so quietly that the judge had to ask her to speak up. So unrelenting was the interrogation that she almost collapsed when stumbling over questions about her possession of morphia and heroin tablets.

Following a two hour summing up from the judge, the jury was out for an equal amount of time before returning at 4.p.m. The foreman announced the verdict to the hushed courtroom:

Guilty of murder with a strong recommendation of mercy.

Dorothea's mother collapsed. Dorothea, supported by two wardresses, betrayed no emotion. When asked by the judge why sentence of death should not be passed she softly replied, her face reddening:

I am innocent.

97. The trial generated enormous interest throughout Nottingham and indeed the country. Here the crowd outside the Shire Hall jostle with the police as they await the verdict.

The judge donned the black cap and, after telling the prisoner the recommendation of mercy would be forwarded to those who advised the Crown, set about his gruesome duty:

You have been convicted of the crime of murder. It only remains for me to pass the sentence which the law requires. It is that you be taken from this place to a lawful prison, and be hanged by the neck until you are dead, and that your body be buried within the precincts of the prison in which you have been confined prior to your prosecution, and may the Lord have mercy upon your soul..

The shocked 'nurse' stared blankly in front of her before being taken down.

The Crown did not proceed with the case of Loisa Baguley, the mother, and both Waddingham and Sullivan were found 'not guilty'. After breaking through police barricades to catch a glimpse of the condemned prisoner, the immense crowds outside the Shire Hall slowly made their way home. Dorothy was transported to what was to be her last home in Birmingham. Ronald Sullivan walked away a free man.

Following the failure of her appeal, shortly before her execution, Dorothea was visited by her mother, sister and Sullivan. The *Daily Express* gave an account of the pathetic meeting:

Separated by a six-foot table, they spoke words of cheer to her.

Nurse Waddingham handed Sullivan her wedding ring, and pictures of himself and the children she had kept by her through the ordeal.

She also gave instructions too for the children's future. Sullivan was on the point of breaking down when he came out.

'Someone has been poisoning her mind against me' he said. She cried, and asked me why I did not do something. She had always been so cheerful before.

Later Sullivan said: 'Nancy (Nurse Waddingham) is the bravest woman I know. She knew it was the last time we might ever meet, but despite this she spent nearly all the time discussing domestic matters, the kiddies future, arrangements for the distribution of the furniture in our home, and many other matters.

Of herself she said little. She is, of course, hoping there will be a respite, but she is resigned to her fate. 'Joe, I am innocent' she said, just before we parted. 'You know it so do many other people. When I first came here after the trial, I strove not to life. Now I am striving to live. Always let the children think well of me. You know I love them.'

As we parted she smiled at me and said "Goodbye Joe. Don't worry. Good luck". I said "Not goodbye, Nancy, just good afternoon. I'll see you again."

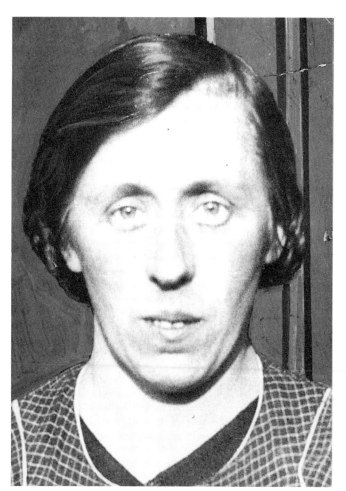

98. 'Nurse' Waddingham protested her innocence until the very end.

In the early hours of Tuesday 16th April 1936, a crowd of up to 12,000 congregated around Winson Green Prison in Birmingham. Some had come to cheer but most to jeer. One of the biggest demonstrations against capital punishment ever witnessed in Britain had been organised by Mrs. Violet Van Der Elst. Defying hundreds of policemen she stood unflinchingly by her Rolls Royce alternately broadcasting hymns and haranguing the crowd. Men paraded through the streets wearing sandwich boards : 'THIS BARBAROUS AGE HANGS THE MOTHER OF FIVE CHILDREN'.

As the hanging hour of 9 o'clock approached who knows what was passing through Dorothea's mind. Perhaps she was making her peace with God, perhaps thinking about her five children - the eldest 11 and youngest 4 months. Maybe, just maybe, she was as innocent as she maintained to the end. Or should somebody have shared the guilt? She stepped firmly to the scaffold. We shall never know.

As a church clock struck nine, the crowd outside fell silent. Every head was bowed. A few women knelt in prayer. There were few dry eyes. The notice of execution was fixed outside the prison gates at 9.04.a.m.

By order of the state five children were deprived of the love of their mother, then dangling at the end of a rope.

A SIMPLE DOMESTIC

99. Stanley Woodcock sentenced to death for the murder of his 25-year-old wife in Plunger Lane, Beechdale Estate in 1948. It was the all too familiar story of young love turning sour. Woodcock became insanely jealous of his wife and in a fit of anger murdered her in the scullery. He then tried to commit suicide by slashing his own throat and turning on the gas taps. He was rescued by a neighbour.

A tragic tale of when young love turns to hatred

SUMMARY: MURDER OF WIFE. INADEQUATE PERSONALITY. REJECTION MOTHER AMBIVALENT MENTAL DISHARMONY. HOSTILE FATHER. SIBLING JEALOUSY.

Thus terminated the routine prison medical officer's report on Stanley Woodcock. His crime did not attract one tenth the coverage in newspapers as that of 'Nurse' Waddingham. To both journalists and police alike, it was just another 'domestic'. Many of us have felt the urge to kill, often the ones we love. Fortunately, only a few carry out this most horrific of crimes, usually in a fit of temper and very much regretted a few minutes later. 25-year-old Marjorie Irene Woodcock was the victim of just such a crime - strangled by her childhood sweetheart/husband, in Plunger Lane, Beechdale Estate in 1948.

The perpetrator of the crime was a sickly child who suffered throughout his life from chronic bronchitis. His father was an irritable and quick-tempered alcoholic who had the worst possible job for a man with such traits - he was a publican. He was dozy and grumpy and had little time for his seven children, showing neither love nor affection for anything other than the bottle.

Stanley's mother was highly-strung, jittery and terrified of her brutish husband. She worked as a barmaid. She was a poor home maker and frequent marital quarrels were played out in front of the children. After drink, the publican was an ugly, domineering man, who negatively affected the lives of all his children before succumbing to TB in 1940.

For some reason that was never properly explained to the prison psychologist, Stanley Woodcock was farmed out as a child to another couple and spent most of his early years away from the family home, returning only at weekends. He could do no wrong in the eyes of his surrogate parents and they accordingly allowed him to have his own way more times than was good for him. When he returned to his family at weekends there were inevitably rows and, at 14, after leaving William Crane School, he returned to live permanently with his natural parents. Feeling a stranger in his own home he was forever clashing with his siblings and parents.

Stanley went to work in the cigarette packing

department at Players and spent weekends with his adopted family, whom he'd now begun to call 'mum' and 'dad'. He keenly felt the rejection of his natural parents. Drafted into the RAF in 1941, he married his childhood sweetheart, Marjorie, the following year. Neither had been out with any other member of the opposite sex.

Following his discharge due to chronic bronchitis in 1945, Woodcock moved back to Nottingham, and was re-employed at Players as a maintenance engineer earning £7.10s. per week. With the couple still residing at Marjorie's mother's home, conditions became untenable when the younger woman gave birth to a son. It was a big relief for all concerned when they moved into their own home. Content to lead a sedate life, Woodcock doted on his son and spent his leisure time pottering about in the house and garden. He neither smoked nor drank and became a 'cardigan and slippers' man at an early age. Marjorie, though, was a very different personality. Used to having her own way she became disenchanted as the years slowly passed. Dull domesticity - with an anorak for a husband - was not the kind of life she'd spent her teenage years daydreaming about. She saw her youth slowly slipping away in the depressing circle that is marriage, mortgage and monotony.

With funds provided by her part-time job at a jewellers, Marjorie started going out in the evenings, to the dance halls and picture houses, anywhere for a little excitement to escape her humdrum existence. She began to taunt her husband with stories, both true and false, of young men she had met.

To the neighbours it seemed a fairly normal marriage, with the usual ups and downs. Behind closed doors, though, there was tension between the lemon and the libertine. Marjorie often complained about her husband's excessive demands for sexual intercourse informing him, in no uncertain terms, that his compulsive advances were not welcome. Clearly there were not the usual ups and downs. There followed a nightly struggle over conjugal rights. Stanley was being rejected a second time, this time by his wife. He became angry and depressed and spent long hours brooding. He was worried she was seeing other men. He knew their marriage was foundering.

Some three weeks before her murder, the feuding couple drew up a separation document. Mrs. Woodcock was to remain in the family home, while her husband was to move out. Maintenance of 22s. 6d. per week, for the son, was agreed on. No other payment would be made. The couple agreed to sell all the contents of the house, except for the three piece suite and one bed.

Stanley, being self-centred and possessive, was becoming more and more frustrated at the

100. Woodcock, an ideal prisoner, was released after serving less than ten years. He left to make a new life for himself in Clevedon.

path his life was taking. For the second time he was being rejected by those he thought should love him. He was being ousted from his home, separated from his child. This was all at his wife's instigation, she was responsible for his rejection. The distressed man decided to have one last try at reconciliation but after arguments lasting the whole of Saturday night and Sunday morning, Marjorie decided she could take no more. She commenced to pack her bags. As the prison medical officer would later suggest:

Woodcock slipped into a state of infantile despair and rage and was urged to drastic action.

Taking a piece of cloth, Stanley knotted it once. Wrapping it round his wife's throat he pulled both ends with the force of a man possessed. Marjorie died of strangulation. She was 25 years old.

When all breath had been squeezed from Marjorie he carried her from the scullery into the bedroom and carefully laid the still warm corpse on the bed. He was determined to join his wife by taking his own life, but the carving knife and razor he chose were not sharp enough for the bloody job. He was found, in a semi-conscious state, by a neighbour in the kitchen with three jets of the gas cooker fully opened. The failed suicide was rushed to hospital and consequently made a complete recovery. He later stated that suicide had been a harder job than he had anticipated.

At the subsequent trial the jury took two hours to find Woodcock guilty of murder. When asked if he had anything to say, the prisoner clutched the dock and in a faltering voice pronounced:

God knows that I have told the truth.

The judge donned the black cap and sentenced the young man to hang.

The prospects for a successful appeal were fairly strong, the murder was not premeditated. The death sentence was repealed and Woodcock was told he would spend the rest of his life in prison.

In gaol he was the object of several reports. Despite never having been in trouble before, he fitted in well to the prison regime and after four years in stir the chaplain reported:

He has responded to spiritual ministrations and seeks atonement for his crime. He is not a criminal type and his attitude towards crime is normal.

The Governor found him a model prisoner:

His conduct has been excellent. Co-operative,

obliging, courteous and well-mannered, he is liked by everyone.

Stanley Woodcock was released in 1957 after serving less than ten years. Shortly before his release the assistant governor observed:

Throughout the whole length of his sentence he has been a model prisoner, cheerful and adaptable. However I feel that the enormity of his crime has never really come home to him, and he is inclined to be a little smug and self-satisfied. He will be making a new life for himself in Clevedon.

Woodcock was released at the discretion of the then Home Secretary, R.A.Butler. Through one irrational fit of pique he had lost his wife, his son (who went to live with Marjorie's parents) and nine years of his liberty. He was also exiled from his home town. For the police and reporters just another 'domestic'. How many readers may be wondering, there but for the Grace of God?

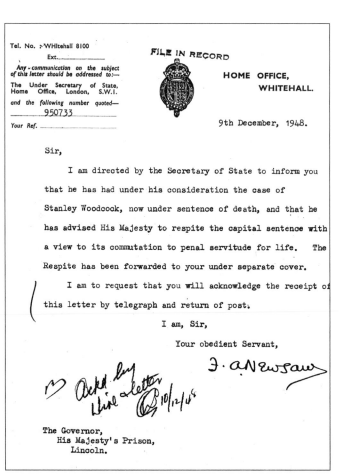

101. The letter from the Home Office which spared Woodcock's life. Only three of the thirty-three murderers apprehended in Nottingham 1945-65 went to the gallows.

'THE PERFECT MURDER'

102. The Roxy Cinema on Ribblesdale Road. It was here that Mabel went to see 'The Baron of Arizona' starring Vincent Price. In the dark seats in the cheapest part of the cinema she had the misfortune to meet the young man who brought her life to a tragic, premature end the following evening.

An obnoxious teenager takes the biggest gamble of his life - with his life!

In the cheapest seats of the darkened Roxy Cinema on Ribblesdale Road a 19-year-old literary poseur from the Meadows, Herbert Mills, whispered to the woman next to him. Aged 48, Mabel Tattershaw was surprised and flattered when the thin blonde teenager, just a few years older than her daughters, suggested a rendezvous, outside the Metropole cinema, the following evening at 6.p.m. on Friday 3rd. August 1951. Losing all interest in Vincent Price and *The Baron of Arizona*, Mabel mentally began making plans for the next day.

Quite who had the biggest shock when they met in the cold light of day is open to conjecture. Mabel, using copious amounts of face-powder and lipstick, had done her best to mask the ravages of a hard life. In her council house on Longmead Drive, Edwards Lane Estate, Mabel had dolled herself up as best she could carefully applying make-up in front of the mirror and putting her dark brown hair into plaits. One of her lodgers, Lillian Wilson later told police: 'She made herself look really nice.' In her handed-down floral dress, Mabel waited apprehensively outside the Metropole on Mansfield Road for her first date with such a young man in many, many years. She fingered her plastic beads nervously, wondering what her husband, who was in prison, would have had to say had he known about the assignation. She was probably made more nervous when she glanced up at the title of the current attraction - *I'll Get You For This.*

Mills, no oil painting himself, but cocky and brash, kept the appointment and the mismatched couple wandered through the side streets of Sherwood, along Mansfield Road, and finally ended up in an overgrown orchard, known locally by courting couples as 'The Jungle'.

As they sat under the clouds, lonely Margaret probably expected the teenager to make some sort of sexual advance. Unfortunately, Herbert Mills was not particularly interested in the normal pursuits of 19-year-old men; he had his own agenda and uppermost on his mind that evening was his

103. Mabel Tattershaw from Longmead Drive. The 48-year-old had met a teenage boy in the cinema and was murdered by him the following evening. Her body was 'discovered' in deep undergrowth off Sherwood Vale about a week later by Herbert Mills - her date for the evening!

fascination with committing the perfect murder. The hapless mother of two teenage daughters was his chosen victim.

After first removing the plastic beads he thought might get in the way, Mills covered Mabel with her own coat. He then coolly knelt on the coat, preventing his victim from moving her arms. Then he put his hands around the terrified woman's neck and squeezed hard. Mabel was powerless to defend herself in any way but somehow managed to pick up some fibres from her assailant's suit, which were later discovered under her nails.

The young murderer, who described himself as an artist and poet, fled the scene of the crime and impatiently waited for the body to be discovered. One day passed, two days, five days, nothing happened. Mills, by now desperate for his fifteen minutes of fame, could wait no longer. From a call box on the junction of Mansfield Road and Villiers Road, Woodthorpe, just after noon on Thursday 9th August, the attention seeking teenager phoned the *News of the World*. He asked them if they were interested in the body of a woman he believed to have been murdered. The crime reporter's ears pricked up when he heard the caller boast:

Even the police don't know about it.

They did a few minutes later. Alerted by the reporter, Norman Rae, detectives were waiting for the braggart as he left the call box! He calmly led them to the derelict orchard between Maurice Avenue and Mapperley Rise and pointed out the body. It had been concealed under a thick clump of hawthorn bushes and was covered with an old grey-brown coat. The blue flowered dress, lisle stockings and brown crepe-soled shoes had not been disturbed. An examination of the pockets revealed a small tin of snuff, a dirty stained piece of underclothing used as a handkerchief, an empty brown leather purse and a clue as to where the victim may have been going - a pair of spectacles which Mrs. Tattershaw wore when going to the cinema. At first glance it appeared that Mabel had died from head wounds inflicted by the fists of her assailant.

Still on probation for theft, Mills was not a complete stranger to police procedure and was questioned throughout the afternoon. He handed over the pathetic plastic bead necklace which he claimed to have found near the body. Mills was a cocky gambler whose Post Office statements of entry and withdrawal showed that he had won and lost very heavily. At one stage he had been £3,800 in credit but now owed the bookmaker £1,000. He planned to sell his story to the newspapers to help pay off his debt. He was making his biggest gamble and the stake was his own life. The odds against him were mounting.

With as yet no concrete evidence against Mills, the police were forced to let the young man go and he was quickly whisked off to London, his expenses and a sightseeing tour being provided courtesy of the *News of the World.* Throughout a long weekend, Mills tried to tempt the accompanying reporter into buying more stories from him by divulging tidbits of information, which were later proven to be lies or details that only the killer could have known.

104. The obnoxious punter and pseudo-poet Herbert Mills arriving at Leen-Side mortuary. He had planned what he considered to be the 'perfect murder' in order to make money by selling his story to the newspapers. He took the ultimate gamble - with his life - and lost!

Mills claimed that he wandered through the countryside reading Shelley and composing his own poetry. His fiction was to become his undoing. He stated that his attention had been drawn to the corpse by a glimpse of a white face. After six days in the undergrowth the face was anything but white. He also stated that he knew that Mabel had been strangled. At the time he said this, the police, doctors and press all believed that the victim had been battered to death.

When strangulation was confirmed as the cause, the finger of suspicion pointed firmly at the man who had discovered the body. Two blond hairs, matching those taken from Mills, were found on the body and fibres identical to those of his suit were discovered under the fingernails. There was no evidence of sexual assault.

105. The Metropole where Mabel met Mills at 6.p.m. on Friday 3rd. August 1951. The mismatched couple were seen wandering around the Sherwood area. Mills coldbloodedly strangled Mabel later that evening. The title of the film showing at the Metropole was 'I'll Get You For This'.

On 23rd August, a detective inspector went to London to discuss the case with the Director of Public Prosecutions. On his return journey on the train, the D.I. met Norman Rae, the *News of the World* reporter, who had taken Mills' initial telephone call. Rae said the young man had phoned again asking for a meeting in the Black Boy Hotel. He was about to make his ultimate gamble.

Mills had been trying to sell his story to other national reporters, hinting he knew a lot more than he'd previously revealed. He also asked about conditions in Broadmoor and stated his belief, erroneously, that people under 21 could not be hanged. It later became clear that Mills' plan was to make a full confession, retract it at the trial and hopefully sell his story for thousands of pounds. He was gambling with his life.

At 8.30.p.m. on 24th August 1951, three weeks after the 'perfect murder', Mills wrote out his confession in the lounge of the Black Boy. It was so long and detailed that more notepaper from the hotel had to be brought in. The confession was not completed until the early hours of the morning. It was handed over to Mr. Rae, and reporter and murderer slept on the statement. The following morning Mills insisted that he stuck by his confession, which was duly passed on to the police. The teenager was promptly arrested. As the statement was handed over Mills commented, referring to the police:

I thought they were making no progress, I decided that I should assist them.

Mills statement concludes with his version of the murder:

...She took off her coat and lay down. I asked could I have the beads she wore. I was interested in plastic, or rather I thought they might interfere with my little crime and intentions. She broke the beads from her neck to give to me. I tied them. She was a very simple woman.

We had spoken on the way there and she had told me of her husband being in prison, also of her daughter having been seduced by the lodger. She had known something of what her daughter was doing, yet did not attempt to interfere in any way. If I had thought of changing my mind, the thought of the daughter quickly altered it. I did not like what had happened. I was satisfied that I had found the perfect victim.

She said she was cold. I had not interfered with her in any way, nor did I. I covered her with her own coat. She had her eyes closed. I put on a pair of gloves. I knelt with my knees upon her shoulders. The coats were placed upon her so that she would not clutch or gather any thread within her finger nails.

I was very pleased. I think I did it rather well. The strangling itself was quite easily accomplished. I am right-handed and I applied most pressure to the right hand side of her neck. I examined the contents of her pockets, which I replaced. I slid down the bank, covered the coat over her, then left, arriving home at, I think, 9.20. p.m.

I have determined to make this statement which I realise involves a charge of murder. I now confess I murdered Mrs. Tattershaw.

Mills, in accordance with his private plan, later retracted this confession but did admit meeting Mabel. He said that he left her alive and well.

I was ashamed to be seen walking with her, so I said, more or less, that I had made a mistake and had better go. She walked away and I went round the corner and got a bus to the Scala Cinema.

At his trial, Mills was described by his own counsel as being *a hateful boy* [whose] *confession was sheer invention, full of bombast and childish vanity, obviously fed on cheap fiction.*

Once two witnesses had testified to having seen the couple together on the evening of the murder no bookmaker would have given odds against the accused being found 'not guilty'. After a four day, trial the jury was out for just 25 minutes. When the death sentence was announced Mills, grinned at both judge and jury.

Murderers often feel themselves compelled to return to the scene of their barbarity. If Mills had returned to the Roxy just two weeks after his act of murder, he would have seen his fate writ large: the film showing was *Convicted*.

Leonard Mills was hanged at Lincoln Prison on 11th December 1951.

Nine years later John Louis Constantine, another young deviant, met the same fate.

UNLOVED AND UNLAMENTED

The sordid story of a young thief, the last man to be hanged for a murder in the city.

On September 1st 1960 two cyclists pedalled past Lincoln Prison. On the pavement nearby, a woman and her schoolboy son wished the postman 'Good morning'. In the same vicinity, nine police officials stood self-consciously by, looking for some kind of crowd to control. Within the walls, scarcely fifty yards away, 23-year-old John Louis

Constantine was making his peace with God. He was the last man condemned to death for a murder committed in Nottingham. The petty thief, for the most part unloved and unlamented, died for a murder he'd committed some five months previously.

Lily Parrie, aged 76 and from the Meadows area, kept a shop selling general provisions and cigarettes. As she was sometimes lonely at night the 15-year-old daughter of a neighbour often slept in the bedroom next to hers above the shop. On St George's day Constantine, with the help of a jemmy, broke a glass panel and entered the premises in search of cigarettes. Choosing the wrong room he stumbled across the elderly owner and unhesitatingly brought the crowbar down on the frail woman's head, fracturing her skull. Constantine made good his escape with £20-30 contained in an imitation snakeskin purse, together with a considerable number of cigarettes. He cast the jemmy into the canal. The following morning the teenage companion saw blood trickling from under the owner's bedroom door. Following an emergency operation the injured woman lived for five days before succumbing to her injuries.

Meanwhile, Constantine was spending his ill-gotten gains on tawdry, trendy superfluities like initialised lighters, a watch and records. Being well known to the police he was automatically interviewed and several packets of cigarettes, known to be from the dead woman's premises, were found in his possession. In a statement, Constantine did not deny that he had taken part in the burglary but insisted that an accomplice had struck the fatal blow. He stuck to this story throughout the trial, despite overwhelming evidence to the contrary. The man accused by Constantine, Brian Walker, had nine witnesses to testify that he was elsewhere that night.

Wearing a light blue suit, white shirt and black and green tie, Constantine occasionally made notes during the process of his trial, but sometimes lost interest. He was observed reading a novel, *Beyond Defeat,* whilst his fate was being decided in the Birmingham court. He remained composed when sentenced to death, but both his young wife and mother sobbed in each other's arms.

They had a strange ally in their belief that the death penalty was too harsh. Normally the police complain about the leniency of many sentences. On this occasion a detective made a plea that the death penalty should be commuted. He had known the condemned man since his childhood and was aware of how badly he had been treated. The plea was supported by other officers, but to no avail.

In Lincoln, the weary schoolboy wound his way to school, the postman sorted his letters and John Louis Constantine dangled from a rope.

SATURDAY NIGHT AND SUNDAY MORNING

The unsolved mystery of the 'Pretty Windows' murder

106. The Fox and Grapes, Sneinton. Known by the locals as 'Pretty Windows'.

Of the 34 murders committed between the end of the war and the abolition of hanging, 33 were detected and three men executed. The 'one that got away' was particularly difficult to solve as there appeared to be no motive. Popularly referred to as the 'Pretty Windows' murder, the file remains open and the mystery is still debated. With most stabbings perpetrated by young men, and the crime committed in 1963, there is a good chance that the guilty party is still alive and maybe walking the streets of Nottingham today.

George Wilson was the highly respected landlord of the Fox and Grapes (commonly referred to as the 'Pretty Windows' because of the ornate glass work) a cosy local near the fruit and vegetable market in Sneinton. As an ex-miner he had been readily accepted by the locals during his eighteen month tenure and was an unlikely victim being a good socialiser with no known enemies.

On Saturday 6th September 1963 the locals were in good spirits. Forest had beaten Wolves 3-0 (Wignall, Quigley and Le Flem) and were later in the month to progress to head the first division table. The Beatles were at No.1 with 'She Loves You' and all was well with the world. The regulars were having a good sing-song before the 10.30.

closing time. By 11.p.m. the pub had been cleared, the doors locked and George, his wife Betty, a trainee couple and a friend settled down in the lounge to unwind with a quiet drink. Just after 11.p.m. there was a knock at the door, probably someone looking for 'afters'. Mary answered but the caller had already left. The trainees departed at 11. 30. and the friend, Mr. Smith, at 12.15. a.m.

George, as was his habit, took the opportunity to both say goodbye and take his pub dog, a rough-haired mongrel, for a walk. Other than the murderer, Blackie was the only witness to the gruesome stabbing a few minutes later which terminated his master's life on his own doorstep.

It is unlikely that George even saw his assailant as the first of fourteen frenzied stabs with a bowie knife penetrated the base of his skull. The following thirteen knife wounds pierced both the front and back of his body and were inflicted with great force and venom, one of the wounds penetrating up to three and a half inches. George had not had the opportunity to defend himself. His keys were found on the pavement next to the body and there had been no attempt at robbery as his money was still in his blood-soaked pockets. Pieces of slate from a low roof nearby were strewn near the corpse. Perhaps the killer had jumped down before the attack.

Blackie, speckled with his master's blood, barked and scratched frantically at the pub door which Betty hastily opened:

The first thing I saw was my husband. It was obvious he was badly injured.

By the time the ambulance arrived the father of two was dead. A murder enquiry was immediately instigated and a police caravan installed near the scene of the crime. Police toured the area with loudspeakers asking for witnesses to come forward and interviewed all the occupants at the nearby Salvation Army hostel. The little evidence available was collated by a massive squad of over 175 police men and women assigned to the case.

At throwing-out time the streets so near to the city centre were full of drinkers some waiting for the paddy bus, others staggering home. The area was well-lit and the success or failure in detecting the murderer was dependent upon somebody having seen something suspicious, or the murder weapon being found and its origin traced.

A driver for a security firm came forward and told officers that he had narrowly avoided running down a man in Longden Street at 12.50.a.m.. The 'running man', as he was to become known, was wearing a green Robin Hood type hat and light coloured raincoat. He appeared to have a chisel in his hand.

Over the coming weeks and months 300 possible suspects had their movements checked and thousands more were interviewed. For the first time the local police asked for assistance from Scotland Yard. Staff at Nottingham hospitals were questioned to see if they had treated the victims of dog bites - it is unclear whether Blackie was able to defend his master. Drains, dustbins and the roofs of neighbouring buildings were painstakingly searched for the murder weapon.

It was October before the police got their first breakthrough. The knife used in the murder was discovered in its sheath in a ditch on the road between Nottingham and Ratcliffe-on-Trent, probably thrown from a passing vehicle. Forensic tests proved conclusively that the police had the murder weapon in their possession. Faint traces of blood matched those of the murder victim. At its tip the blade was bent and when it was extracted from the body it acted like a hook on the landlord's clothes, picking up strands from his shirt and jacket. When put back in its sheath after the murder, the strands became detached and locked in the sheath until discovered by forensic scientists. The investigators now had their weapon but were still puzzled as to the motive.

A detailed examination of Mr. Wilson's lifestyle revealed no obvious enemies. He was not in debt and no evidence was found of any extra-marital affairs. At the inquest it was revealed that, two months before the murder, George had received an anonymous death threat, but why should anyone wish to murder a jovial, friendly family man with no known enemies?

Several theories were mooted, the most popular being that George had stumbled across a burglar, or even a gang, about to break into the pub. The burglar panicked and slashed out with the deadly blade. The police had been tipped off that the Fox and Grapes was on the hit-list of a gang of Scottish burglars operating in Nottingham. The gang and their associates were all cross-questioned but no information was forthcoming.

A second theory was that George was killed by a passing maniac and the ferocity of the attack certainly supported this supposition.

A third line of enquiry pursued the idea that George had been murdered in a case of mistaken identity. The previous landlord was of similar build and sometimes took his dog for a walk late at night.

At least five people confessed to the slaying. A man from Radford, imprisoned in Dartmoor and serving a life sentence for killing an inmate in the prison, asked to see a detective from Nottingham. When at liberty he had confessed to the murder and later retracted the confession. Now, after having committed a murder, he wanted to get the second one off his chest. He began scribbling his written confession and finished eight pages later. When examined by the visiting detective it was found to contain details that only the murderer could have known. He recounted that he had been in the Fox and Grapes the evening of the murder and had argued with the landlord about the afternoon's football match between Forest and Wolves. George had made a few jokes at Forest's expense, whose funny side the prisoner, a Forest fanatic, could not see. He left the hostelry in a huff, continued his pub crawl in town and came across George some time after midnight. Seeing red, the fan made a vicious attack on his tormentor, before calmly walking home. The next day he threw the knife away during the course of a ride he had thumbed to Radcliffe The story sounded plausible until the prisoner was asked to identify George Wilson from a set of photographs. He was also shown a variety of knives and could identify neither the knife nor the victim. The confession was dismissed as were several others using the same methods.

A second suspect came into the picture after police revealed details of the exact location of where the knife was discovered. On September 11th, just a few days after the murder, a hitch-hiker was picked up at almost the same spot as where the knife was later found. He never came forward although the motorist gave a comprehensive description and remembered some of their conversation.

The man was about 30, thin, 5' 8" with receding auburn hair, brushed back. He was wearing glasses with no lower rim, a college scarf and a raincoat with a small gold cross in his lapel. They had an eclectic conversation covering topics as diverse as chiropody and monasteries. Hardly the sort of subject matter for somebody who had just dumped a murder weapon, but the police were anxious to follow every lead.

With the passage of time the trail grew colder. The police did not get the lucky break that is needed in motiveless crime. Like in every unsolved case there are those, including policemen, in Nottingham, who are said to know the identity of the murderer, but cannot or will not prove their suspicions. At least one man does know the guilty party - that is if he hasn't taken his secret to the grave.

Mrs. Wilson and her 10-year-old son and 6-year-old daughter moved away from the area. An anonymous letter arrived later instructing her to go to Derby bus station with £100 to discover the identity of the killer. She missed the rendezvous. Subsequent landlords have received anonymous telephone calls warning them that they would be next. Somehow the case just will not die.

Nottingham 1910

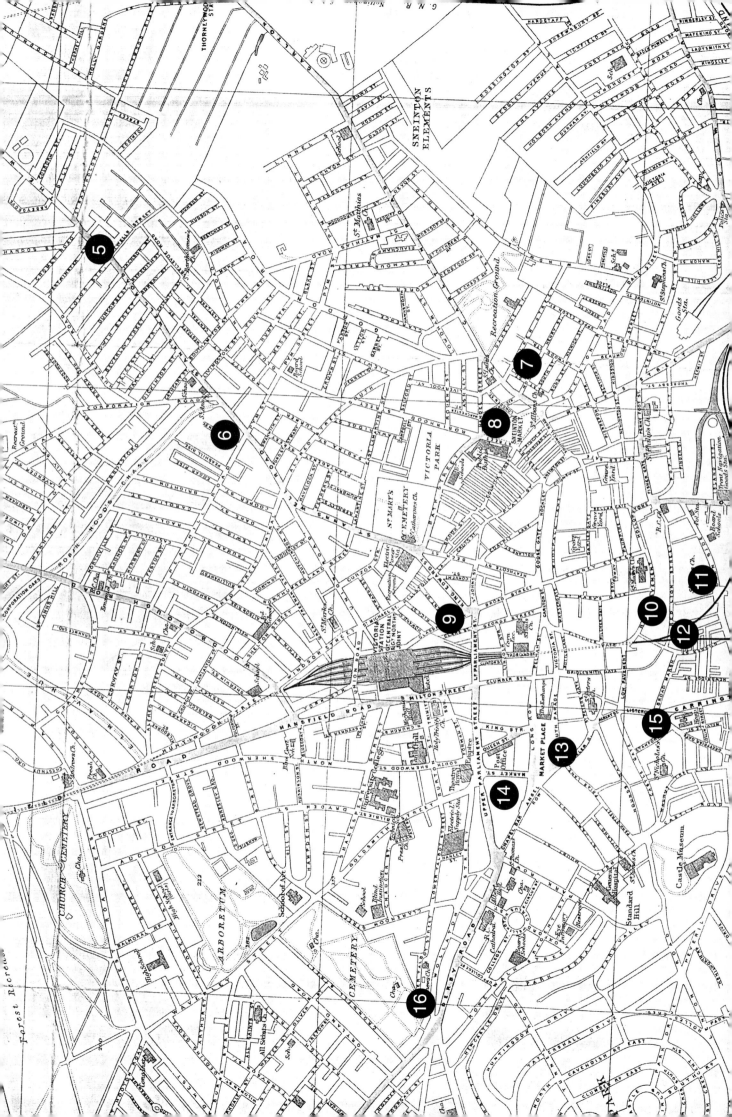

WICKED NOTTINGHAM

(1) Bagthorpe Prison opened in November, 1891. All prisoners were transferred from the County Gaol and the St. John's Street Prison. The following fifteen murderers were hanged here. Nearly every case concerns the murder of a woman by a man known to her.

27th March 1894 Walter Smith (p78)

26th March 1895 Edmund Kesteven for the slashing with a razor of Sarah Oldham at Sutton.

24th December 1895. Henry Wright for the brutal murder of Mrs. Reynolds and her two sons in Mansfield.

11th August 1896 John Rose (p79)

11th August 1896 Samuel Wilkinson (p79)

23rd December 1896 Joseph Allcock (p79)

9th August 1899 Elias Torr for the murder of his wife in Hickling.

29th March 1905 John Hutchinson (p72)

7th August 1906 Edward Glynn (p80)

14th December 1909 Samuel Atherley (p80)

7th April 1922 Percy Atkins buried his wife alive in an allotment in Derby.

8th August 1923 Albert Burrows for the murder of Anna Calladine and her child in Derby.

17th December 1924 Arthur Simms for the murder of Rose Armstrong.

27th April 1927 William Knighton for the murder of his mother.

10th April 1928 George Haywood for the murder of Amy Collinson in Derbyshire.

(2) Villiers Road, just off the map. It was from a telephone kiosk at the junction with Mansfield Road that Mills telephoned the *News of the World* to inform them he had 'found' a body.

(3) Mabel Tattershaw's body was 'discovered' in the derelict orchard between Maurice Avenue and Mapperley Rise.

(4) Devon Drive, home of 'Nurse' Waddingham and scene of the murders of the Baguley's in 1935.

(5) St Ann's Well Road where Henry Westby shot his father on a night of double murder.

(6) The race riots in 1958 were centred around the junction of Peas Hill Road and St. Ann's Well Road.

(7) South Street, the home of the deranged preacher, John Jackson, who enticed young women into his rooms and attempted to rape them. He later prayed that they should be made pure.

(8) Sneinton Market, location of the still unsolved 'Pretty Windows' murder in 1963.

(9) Site of the St. John's Street Prison, one of the places of execution in Victorian times, first used in 1878 for the hanging of John Brooks.

(10) The Shire Hall, scene of Nottingham's last public execution. The County Gaol was located at the rear.

(11) The infamous Narrow Marsh area.

(12) Site of the Narrow Marsh murder of 1905.

(13) Goose Fair, when held in the Market Square, attracted pickpockets from all over the country.

(14) Prostitution was rife in the city centre in the 1860s. It was difficult to walk the streets without being accosted.

(15) Collin Street, site of one of the estimated fifty brothels. Here Elizabeth Raynor grew fat on her profits as a madam. On her fourth appearance in court she was sentenced to one month's hard labour.

(16) Derby Road, where Gypsy Lee was on the knock for gullible housewives.

107. *The Red Lion Inn on Red Lion Street.*

108. *Children watching the demolition of some of their homes, once again In Narrow Marsh.*

109. *Typical Nottingham housing scene in 1952. Almost certainly St Ann's, at least one person can tell us.*

110. Bed & breakfast at the County Gaol (from The Galleries of Justice).

ACKNOWLEDGEMENTS

Viv Foster and I have arguments and we always will. I have to admit that she is right 90 per cent of the time and does an excellent job tidying up the text.

Steve Arnold (who I met serving a long sentence at Ellis Guilford) has an excellent eye for detail and helped enormously with the all too important last minute rewrites.

Staff in both the Nottingham Central Library and at the archives have gone out of their way to help me. Any writer will substantiate my claim that a good librarian and first-class photographer (Dave Bradbury of Wheel Publications) make for a good read.

ILLUSTRATION ACKNOWLEDGEMENTS

NOTTINGHAM LOCAL STUDIES LIBRARY
1,2,3,4,44,46,47,48,51,53,58,62,64,65,66, 67,69,71,72,73,74,75,77,79,80,81,87,88, 102,104,105,106,107,108,109,110.

NOTTINGHAM ARCHIVES
16,17,18,19,20,21,22,23,24,25,27,28,29 ,30,31,32,33,34,35,36,37,38,39,40,41,42, 43,45,55,56,57,59,60,61,63,76,78,82,85,86.

POPPERFOTO
92,93,94,96,97,98,103.

THE PUBLIC RECORD OFFICE
99,100,101.

THE GALLERIES OF JUSTICE, NOTTINGHAM.
90,95,110.

ALL OTHER PHOTOS/ILLUSTRATIONS FROM THE AUTHOR'S COLLECTION.

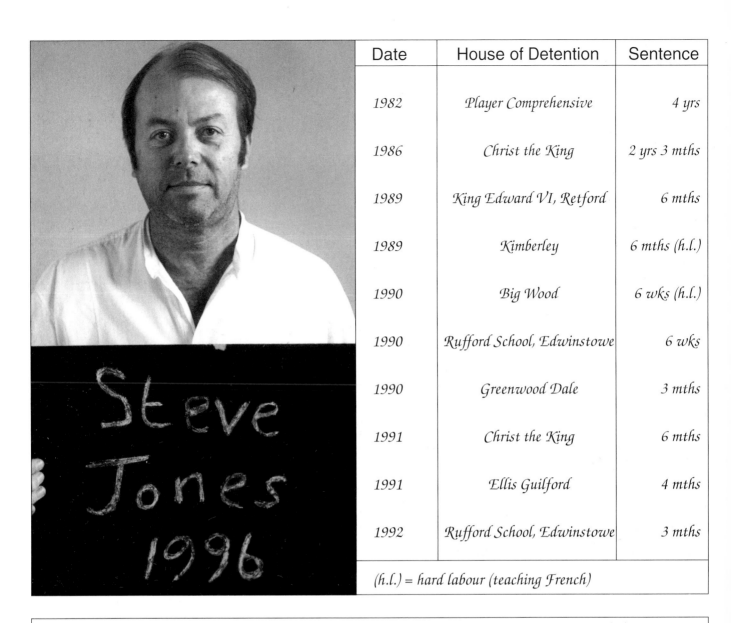

Date	House of Detention	Sentence
1982	Player Comprehensive	4 yrs
1986	Christ the King	2 yrs 3 mths
1989	King Edward VI, Retford	6 mths
1989	Kimberley	6 mths (h.l.)
1990	Big Wood	6 wks (h.l.)
1990	Rufford School, Edwinstowe	6 wks
1990	Greenwood Dale	3 mths
1991	Christ the King	6 mths
1991	Ellis Guilford	4 mths
1992	Rufford School, Edwinstowe	3 mths

(h.l.) = hard labour (teaching French)

Wicked Publications *Presents*

(1) London . . . The Sinister Side

Reprinted every year since 1986.
Includes chapters on Jack the Ripper,
The Kray Twins, executions, the
hangmen of London, prisons. If you
are interested in the darker side of
London's history, its ghosts, murderers,
mystery and misery, then join us in
our trip through
London...The Sinister Side.

See next page for other publications

(2) Wicked London
Murder 'Orrible Murder, the Blitz, early operations and the darker side of everyday life.

(3) London Through the Keyhole
Reveals secrets previously guarded behind locked doors, nineteenth century divorce cases, illicit love affairs, prostitution and night life.

(4) Capital Punishments
These wicked tales of yesteryear are centred around crime, domestic violence and prison conditions in Victorian London. Including sections on juvenile crime, dangerous women, the lighter side of court life and women in prison.

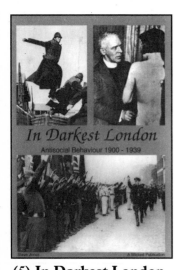

(5) In Darkest London
Prostitutes, criminals, backstreet abortionists, strikers and the police give lengthy accounts of their activities in a frank and unsentimental look at London life from the death of Victoria to the outbreak of the Second World War

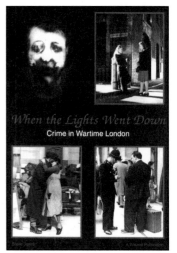

(6) When the Lights Went Down
Many took the opportunities presented by the War to help themselves rather than their country. Murderers, black-marketers, prison-officers and ARP workers talk about their war.

All books are A4 with approximately 80 photographs/illustrations to supplement the wicked tales of yesteryear.

222 Highbury Road, Bulwell, Nottingham NG6 9FE
Tel: (0115) 9756828 or London (0181) 311 3888